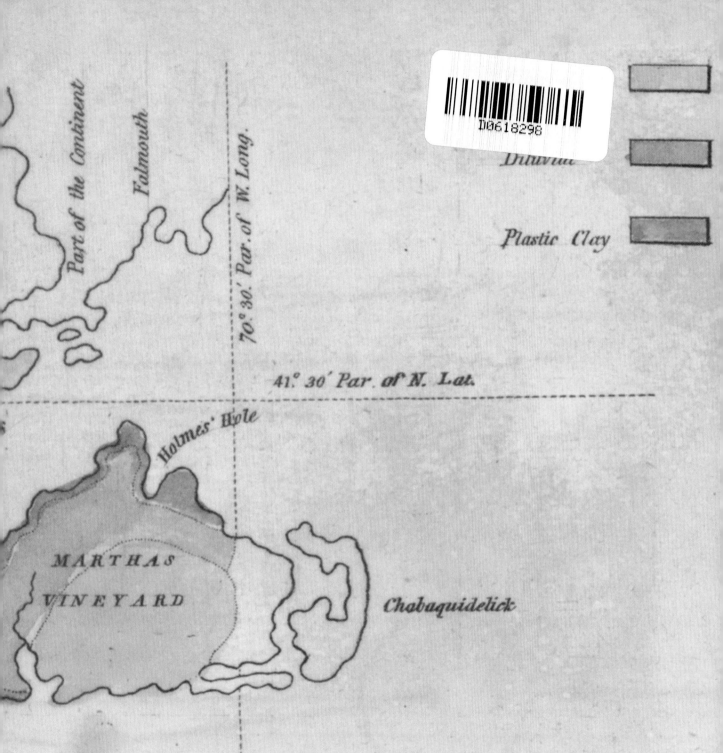

Part of the Continent

Falmouth

70° 30' Par. of W. Long.

41° 30' Par. of N. Lat.

Holmes' Hole

MARTHAS VINEYARD

Chabaquidelick

Diluvial

Plastic Clay

A. Doolittle sc.

the
Beetlebung Farm

cookbook

the Beetlebung Farm cookbook

A Year of Cooking on Martha's Vineyard

Chris Fischer
with Catherine Young

Photographs by Gabriela Herman

Design & Letterpress by Emma Young

LITTLE, BROWN AND COMPANY
New York   Boston   London

Little, Brown and Company
Hachette Book Group
1290 Avenue of the Americas, New York, NY 10104
littlebrown.com

First Edition: May 2015

Little, Brown and Company is a division of Hachette Book Group, Inc.
The Little, Brown name and logo are trademarks of Hachette Book Group, Inc.

The publisher is not responsible for websites (or their content) that are not owned by the publisher.

The Hachette Speakers Bureau provides a wide range of authors for speaking events. To find out more, go to www.hachettespeakersbureau.com or call (866) 376-6591.

ISBN 978-0-316-40407-5
Library of Congress Control Number: 2014957428

10 9 8 7 6 5 4 3 2 1

SC

Printed in China

This book is dedicated to
my Aunt Marie.

CONTENTS

Signs of Spring

Longer Days

High Summer

FOREWORD

Chris Fischer is a cook who farms, a grower who is a talented chef—a brilliant combination. His wonderful recipes celebrate ingredients without getting preachy or precious, in this personal journal of a year cooking on the island he calls home.

We met when construction on The Spotted Pig dragged and I lent a hand in the Babbo kitchen. Chris was working the pasta station then and I noticed his hustle. I got to know him when The Spotted Pig opened. We were always packed—with locals, chefs, celebrities, and anyone else who could squeeze in. Chris would come after work with Mario Batali. They'd head upstairs, crank the radio, and set to shaking off a busy shift with plates of gnudi and lots to drink. Soon Chris would be grabbing chairs and ordering another round for the growing party. Chris is generous with what he holds dear and happiest exchanging stories with friends at a full table.

After his mother died Chris went home to farm with his grandfather. We kept in touch through the lovely vegetables he began delivering. He'd arrive with dirt from the fields on his knees and boxes of the best from the farm and woods. He became a farmer but never stopped cooking. Chris applied to the Rome Sustainable Food Project, Alice Waters's program that brings talented Americans to Europe to cook for scholars at the American Academy. Chris spent part of the winter in a city where reverence for food is a birthright. It was pivotal for him. So was what he did next. He went to London and worked mornings at St. John Bread and Wine and evenings at The River Café. Both do unpretentious food but move ordinary to extraordinary through attention to details. I also cooked at The River Café, so I know Chris was surrounded by kindred souls, working to celebrate the finest ingredients. He was inspired and brought that inspiration home, where he has figured out a way to put it all together. I am so glad he has taken time to share.

April Bloomfield

INTRODUCTION

My grandparents moved to Chilmark in the 1950s. They didn't travel far, but they entered a different world—at least that's how it seemed to my grandfather, whose family had lived on Martha's Vineyard for more than 250 years. But Chilmark was where they wanted to settle, start a family, and buy a farm. So Albert and Regina left the bustle of down-island life and headed up-island to wild, windy pastures and wooded hillsides, where the electric lines were newly strung and most roads weren't paved.

This island is not big, about eighty-eight square miles in total. But it contains many worlds, some that overlap and some that never touch. Chilmark is a rural town in the southwest crook of the island, bounded by Aquinnah at the western tip, Menemsha and Vineyard Sound on the north, and the Atlantic Ocean to the south. My grandfather bought a five-acre parcel at the juncture of Middle Road, South Road, and Menemsha Crossroad—Beetlebung Corner. Like the intersection, his farm was named for the resilient native hardwood tree (known elsewhere as black gum).

The advance, then retreat, of the last ice age created Martha's Vineyard, carved its terrain, and defined its land. The subsequent rise of sea levels separated us from the mainland. Today, particularly up-island, rocks are scattered everywhere. Giant boulders hide in the woods, cluster along the shore, and disappear into the water—all reminders of the enormous climatic and geologic upheaval. Settlers used the mid-sized rocks to build fences to contain the sheep they raised in numbers so large that the forests disappeared for a time. My grandfather, like his forefathers, had to clear tons of stone before he could plant his crops. He hauled some, then blasted the rest with dynamite.

By the time I was a kid, the island's sheep were mostly gone and the woods had grown back around the crumbling hand-piled walls. I grew up in Chilmark—I left and then I came back. I returned after my mother died because I needed to be here and because I wanted to learn how to farm from my grandfather. I had become a cook while I was away; I worked in restaurants in big cities on both coasts of this country and in Europe. So I farmed days and made money nights as a private chef.

I found it surprisingly easy to leave the field and have a meal prepared by sundown, because the ingredients here are so fine they are best almost left alone. I realized then what I had always instinctively known, that the food we grow, the fish we catch, the animals we hunt, and those we raise on grasses and flowers salted by the sea breeze are special because of this place.

That's why I started hosting dinners on Beetlebung Farm. We served what we grew and what our friends caught and raised. The fare was simple, the evenings were informal, no two meals were the same and it was lots of work, but each dinner was a magical occasion.

Then I was offered the job as chef of the Beach Plum Inn & Restaurant in 2013. I accepted, eager for the chance to expand the circle. I began by ripping a hole in the wall between the small kitchen and the old dining room so the kitchen team could see people eating their food and the diners could see us cooking, carefully and with full attention. I continued to manage the farm and used my work there to inspire the menus I wrote every day. We harvested then cooked simply, letting the ingredients shine.

I grew up eating this way. Our meals were planned after a visit to the garden or when my dad got back from fishing. Of course we also made sure to feed the freezer for the cold months — a necessity here. We were not inclined to spend hard-earned money on imported out-of-season vegetables. Frozen peas and canned tomatoes, our own or store-bought, were just fine until the warm weather returned. I still eat this way, enjoying what is best from the farm when I can but happy to open a can, package, or jar when I need to.

I've now been back almost ten years and still marvel at all that this island has to offer. This book celebrates all we have. It is a journal of the past year, the story of the seasons told as I experienced them through seventeen meals I cooked beginning in the warm days after the island emptied and ending a year later when the garden was once again full.

The menus are a collection of recipes that I cooked and ate. Look to them for inspiration but don't feel bound. These are all dishes I will make again and again, likely giving each a tweak every time I do — to suit the season, yes, but also because that is part of the fun.

CF
Martha's Vineyard, 2014

L. iris small
nose heavily fr
hair grey with
lip line very s

Ozzie.
May '72
MMurphy

SECRET SUMMER

OYSTERS,
SAUSAGE

griddled
SQUID
parsley, romesco

wood - grilled
SEA BASS
and salad

PEACHES
for dessert

BEETLEBUNG

FARM

september tenth

POPPY'S FARM

My grandfather was ninety-six years old when he died. He tripped, a bucket of fertilizer in one hand and a shovel in the other, leaving him no way to break his fall. I saw the ambulance as I pulled into the farm with gas for the rototiller. At the hospital his surgeon told us, "Trying to repair Ozzie's hip is like trying to put a screw into quicksand." But we kept our hopes up anyway, until he fell again attempting to get back to the farm.

Poppy, that's what we all called him, passed away three weeks before the Agricultural Fair. He died at home with Gaga (my grandmother, Rena) and their four children by his side. We picked the flowers and vegetables he'd planned to enter then drove it all to the new Ag Hall and submitted everything in his name. He'd always won ribbons; they hung on his walls and filled drawers; he liked to use them as bookmarks. That August, Poppy's farm, Beetlebung, won again, taking top honors for his proud shallots, plump blackberries, and vibrant dahlias.

Beetlebung Farm lies between Middle Road and South Road at Beetlebung Corner in Chilmark. It is nestled on flat land at the foot of pastured hills dominated by the Keith Farm. A small pond sits centered on the groomed acres framed by stone walls dressed in generations of lichen. Those fields and meadows, now in conservation, will remain as they are, which Poppy liked to remind me was not at all how they started when he began working for Mr. Keith in the forties. Poppy cleared then cared for those pastures, supervised the digging of the pond, and reconstructed the crumbling walls built a century before to hold sheep — when they outnumbered people on the island.

It took him many seasons to get rid of the large oaks, then the brush, and finally the stones, until the grass could grow again. He never had the tools he needed; his tractor didn't have a bucket for years, and when he finally upgraded, he got a machine with lights, which meant he could work at night. And he did, night after night, until he drove into a tree, smashing the machine's headlights. After that he determined it was best to once again take the evenings off.

He earned enough working for the Keith family to buy Beetlebung Farm from Robert Vincent in 1961. Although he had entered adulthood with a degree in agriculture, then spent half a lifetime farming, it wasn't until Poppy was forty-six that he finally had land of his own on the island where his family had lived since

1670. He continued working for the Keiths, and on other properties around Chilmark, as he raised his family. He spent as much time as he could with his kids, and in his "spare time" he planted and tended his five-acre plot. Poppy put in the vegetable garden just outside his back door and sowed fields of wildflowers. His daughter Marie helped him plant and tend greens and vegetables in the larger fields.

Poppy's garden was always planted densely, first with peas, onions, and shallots, as soon as the ground could be worked. Then came beets, carrots, lettuce, and potatoes. As the days grew longer and the crowds began to arrive, he would plant his beans, tomatoes, green peppers, and eggplant, the rows in the garden supplementing those in the field. He got his tomato cages ready early, all neatly lined up like soldiers, months before the plants would go into the ground. Then began the countdown of days until his vines boasted ripe beauties. Anticipation, he often said, was his favorite part of farming.

For his eightieth birthday Poppy got a new tractor. Gaga drove it down the driveway, presenting her husband with the well-planned surprise, a small orange Kubota with an automatic transmission. It was the perfect tractor for him. But the shiny new machine didn't replace his old wheel hoe for smaller jobs. Before the weeds could take hold in his aisles, he'd scratch away at the soil, gripping bicycle handlebars attached to a large wheel, metal prongs hanging off the back like the talons of a red-tailed hawk.

He always spoke to his plants, sometimes gently and sometimes not. Over the course of his life as a farmer, many decades cultivating different patches of earth, Poppy created a language and he used it to tell his plants his hopes and expectations, always confident of their response. He famously yelled at a rose bush one summer for not flowering, bringing to mind an agrarian Billy Martin (although he lived in Red Sox country, Poppy always kept the radio tuned to Yankees games). He threatened to cut down the "damn thing" if it didn't start blossoming. After that Poppy boasted, "It bloomed every year." It still does.

Poppy worked Beetlebung Farm for over fifty summers; the topsoil deepened and enriched each one of those years. He and Gaga always woke early and had breakfast as he scanned the sports pages of the *Globe* and she watched the news with the volume off. When their coffee cups were empty, he'd lace up his boots and, rain or shine, head out to the garden. He moved slower as his aches and pains grew, and grudgingly carried a walking stick when his balance betrayed him, but out he'd go, long-brimmed cap on his head, diligently off to work.

Gaga loves asparagus. She likes it best cooked in butter and served on toast. I helped Poppy plant a new row alongside his established crop the year before he died. I dug straight enough to satisfy him, using a long string tied to rebar on each end, pulled taut to keep it true. He supervised from his lawn chair. After we planted, Poppy confessed that he'd let the asparagus plants know he wasn't sure how much longer he'd be around. He'd spoken up, he said, so they'd get to work. The plants answered. The next spring we harvested especially stout and delicious asparagus. We ate them together, mostly on toast.

Sausage in Grape Leaves with Oysters on the Half Shell

Makes about 20

We make sausage on the farm with our own Berkshire pork, which contains a healthy amount of fat; even so, we add a little extra. Once you get the mix made and seasoned, cook up a bit of it, taste it, and adjust the seasoning as necessary. Wrapping the sausage in grape leaves keeps the meat moist. I use wild leaves, but store-bought brined leaves work just as well.

About 2 tablespoons extra-virgin olive oil

1¼ heaping teaspoons fennel seeds (freshly gathered are best!)

1 small clove garlic, chopped

Generous pinch crushed red pepper

1 pound ground pork

¼ pound fresh or cured pork fat, chilled and cut into small dice

Kosher salt

Freshly ground black pepper

About 20 fresh grape leaves (or thoroughly rinsed brined leaves), plus a few extra just in case

1 lemon, cut into eighths

12 oysters in the shell, preferably from nearby, shucked

Heat a little oil in a skillet over medium heat. Add the fennel seeds, garlic, and red pepper and toast until fragrant and the garlic begins to color, about 2 minutes. Spoon the fennel-seed mixture onto a cutting board and roughly chop.

Put the ground pork and fat in a bowl. Season with salt and pepper and add the chopped fennel-seed mixture. Mix well, then cover the bowl and refrigerate for at least an hour.

Bring a pot of lightly salted water to a boil over high heat. Blanch the grape leaves until they wilt, about 30 seconds, then drain and refresh in ice water. Drain the leaves again, gently squeezing out any excess water, and reserve.

(Blanching is not necessary if you are using brined leaves — just rinse them well.)

Roll the sausage in the blanched leaves: put a spoonful of sausage mix in the center, fold, then roll the leaf around the meat. The leaf-wrapped sausage can be cooked immediately, refrigerated for up to a day, or even frozen.

To cook, heat a skim of oil in a heavy-bottomed skillet (large enough to hold the leaves in a single layer) over medium heat. Put the stuffed leaves in the pan and cook gently, lowering the heat if necessary to keep things cooking but not sputtering. Turn the stuffed leaves every 2 to 3 minutes or so and cook until the sausage inside is firm and cooked through, about 10 minutes. Cover the pan and let the leaves rest in the pan juices for about 3 minutes. Serve immediately (or let cool, then reheat in a dry skillet or over the grill) with lemon wedges and chased with freshly shucked oysters.

Griddled Squid

Serves 4

Squid tend to make their way in numbers through Edgartown and Menemsha harbors in the spring and fall, with striped bass in hot pursuit. During the day the squid lie low, but at night they swim toward the water's surface, attracted by moonlight, starlight, and harbor lights, and there lies the secret. A flashlight, a bucket, and a simple squid jig are all you need for an easy night of fishing.

> 4 squid, about 1½ pounds, cleaned (see Note)
>
> About 3 tablespoons neutral oil, such as canola
>
> Kosher salt
>
> About ½ cup loosely packed parsley leaves
>
> 2 tablespoons finely chopped chives
>
> ½ teaspoon minced lemon zest
>
> ½ teaspoon minced garlic
>
> Juice of 1 lemon
>
> About ½ cup Romesco Sauce (page 10)

Rinse the squid bodies, then slice them open and lay them flat. If you are using larger squid, score the bodies, making crosshatch incisions that cut almost, but not quite, through the flesh. Toss both the tentacles and bodies with a little oil and then season them generously with salt.

Heat a griddle or cast-iron pan over high heat. When the griddle or pan is very hot, brush the surface with oil. It will begin to smoke. Add the squid (in batches if necessary), laying the bodies and tentacles in a single layer. Flatten the bodies by weighting them (you can use the bottom of a skillet or a flat lid). Cook the squid until it begins to firm, about 10 seconds, then flip both the bodies and tentacles and cook until they are opaque and tender, about 10 seconds more. Transfer the squid to a bowl.

Toss the squid with the parsley, chives, lemon zest, and garlic, then season again with salt if necessary and finish with lemon juice. Drizzle Romesco Sauce over the squid and serve.

Note: To clean squid, separate the tentacles from the bodies. Remove and discard the beak, guts, ink sack, and quill from the bodies; cut away the eyes. Then rinse the squid thoroughly in cold water.

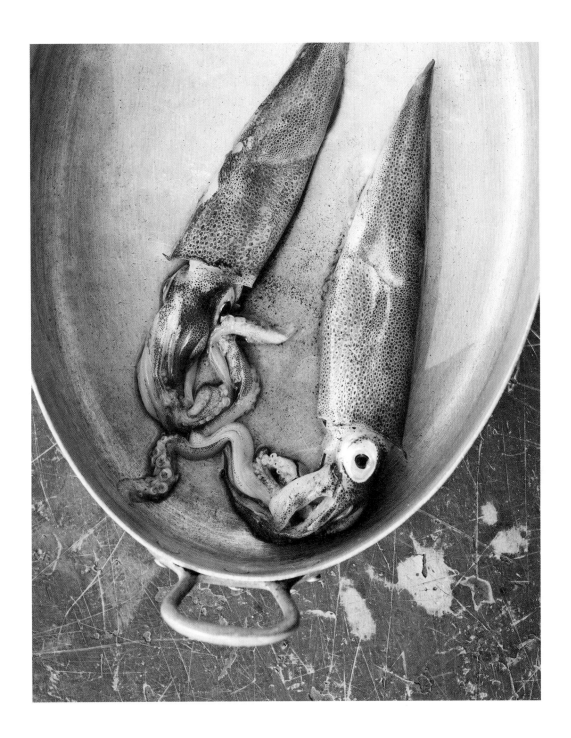

Romesco Sauce

Makes 2 to 3 cups

Romesco Sauce is tart, spicy, and deeply flavored by roasted and charred vegetables. It is good any time of year, but best in September when the peppers, tomatoes, and eggplant are at their peak. The recipe makes enough so you'll have some left over — keep it in the refrigerator and use over the next week or two. I like romesco with poultry as well as fish, and love it with potatoes, particularly Potatoes Crisped in Olive Oil (page 33).

 1 onion, quartered

 1 tomato, quartered

 ½ cup walnuts

 ½ cup slivered almonds

 1 small Japanese eggplant

 2 red peppers

 1 pickled Anaheim or other spicy pepper, stem removed, plus about
   1 tablespoon of the pickling liquid

 1 clove garlic, minced

 About ½ cup extra-virgin olive oil

 Zest of ½ lemon, minced

 1 teaspoon thyme leaves

 About 2 tablespoons sherry vinegar

 Kosher salt

Heat the oven to 400°F. Put the onion and tomato on a baking sheet and roast until they are soft and browned, turning them over once or twice, about 15 minutes in all. Toast the walnuts and almonds in a skillet over medium-low heat until they are slightly colored and fragrant, about 5 minutes.

Char the eggplant on all sides over a hot grill (a stove burner also works) until the skin is burned and it "deflates" and softens, about 5 minutes. When it is cool enough to handle, scoop the flesh into a food processor (or blender). Cook the peppers over an open flame until they are charred all over, also 5 minutes or so, then put them in a sealed container and let them cool. Peel and seed the peppers, then put them in the food processor with the eggplant. Add the onion, tomato, and toasted nuts.

Pulse the food processor. Add the pickled pepper and half of the pickling liquid. Add the garlic and 6 tablespoons of oil. Pulse again, adding additional oil, until the puree is smooth. Add the lemon zest, thyme, vinegar, and salt. Pulse once or twice more, then taste and adjust the seasoning as necessary with pickling liquid, vinegar, and salt. Thin the sauce with a little water so it is pourable and serve immediately or refrigerate.

Grilled Sea Bass

Serves 4

If you are grilling a larger fish, you'll want to cook over lower heat for a longer time. Always test for doneness by sticking a knife in the thickest part of the fish—along the spine. If the flesh looks opaque and separates easily from the bone, the fish is ready to come off the heat.

2 sea bass, each about 2 pounds, scaled and gutted

About 3 tablespoons extra-virgin olive oil, plus a high-quality fruity extra-virgin to finish

Kosher salt

8 lemon wedges

Build a fire in a grill and let it cook down to medium-high heat. Rub the grill with a little oil. Rub the fish all over with oil, then season them well inside and out with salt. Put the fish on the grill and cook until the skin chars and shows grill marks, about 8 minutes. Carefully flip with a spatula. Cook on the other sides until the skin chars and the flesh near the backbone of each is opaque and begins to pull away from the spine, about 8 minutes more. If the fish need more time to cook through, move them to a cool part of the grill, cover with a piece of aluminum foil, and let them "roast" on the grill until they are done. (If it is easier, you can finish cooking the fish in a hot oven, just until the flesh is opaque—a few minutes.) Once they are done, allow the fish to rest for about 2 minutes. Fillet or serve whole, drizzled with olive oil and accompanied by fresh lemon.

SERENA'S SALAD

Soon after my grandparents moved to Beetlebung Farm, Poppy built my grandmother a beauty shop from an unused chicken coop. Serena Modigliani got her hair done there. Like many of Rena's clients, she would stop by the farm stand afterwards to buy armfuls of flowers and vegetables. That's how she got to know my Aunt Marie. Although Serena and my aunt were born years and worlds apart, they became friends because they shared a taste for good food and a love of perfect greens.

Serena grew up in Bologna. She came to this country when she and her husband, an esteemed economist, fled the war racing across Europe. When he joined the faculty at MIT, they bought a home on North Road overlooking Vineyard Sound. I met Serena when I was in my teens and she was in her eighties. I cut her lawn and trimmed trails through her woods that led to bush after healthy bush of wild blueberries. Serena made a wonderful chunky jelly from those berries that she'd share with me because she knew that, like Marie, I loved good food.

I learned many things form Serena, including how to properly make a salad. She was very fond of the greens mix Marie sold. In those days Marie tended toward a combination of mustard greens, red Russian kale, several types of lettuce, and mizuna, all picked quite young before the spiciness of the mustards got too intense. She finished each bag with fennel fronds, nasturtium flowers, and fresh leaves and blossoms from the herb garden. Serena began my lesson by emptying a bag of the cleaned greens into an over-sized salad bowl. "It has to be big," she explained, "you need plenty of room to toss."

"The most important thing," Serena declared, "is to toss the salad one thousand times; always with your hands." She demonstrated the proper technique, lightly making her way beneath the greens in the bowl. "Use a gentle touch, as if you are slipping your hands beneath a sleeping baby that you need to move but don't want to wake." She spread her fingers and lifted the leaves a few at a time, letting them fall gently off in all directions, working slowly and evenly, her palms cupped slightly. "Do this once or twice before you add anything," she instructed. This helps separate the greens and allows cramped leaves to spread: "it's like fluffing a pillow."

Once the greens were "awake," she supervised as I started slowly drizzling olive oil—pouring from a good distance above the bowl, so as not to bruise the leaves. The salad gained a little weight as the oil began to coat. Serena said that from this point onward you shouldn't move your fingers at all. "Allow gravity to do its job and let the leaves settle where they want. And don't add too much oil, just a light kiss on each leaf." Vinegar was next: just enough to liven things. Cheap red wine vinegar was her preference, it thinned the oil just enough to help the leaves dance and slide in the bowl.

Serena would give another spritz of oil and sprinkle of vinegar, taste a leaf, offer me one, and adjust until it was right in her mind—the leaves had their dignity and shape but acknowledged the presence of their veil of dressing, the vinegar a subtle but exciting accent. We'd lightly salt the salad then gently toss it once or twice more before eating it together—the perfect mid-afternoon snack.

Serena exaggerated when she advised tossing a thousand times, but it is not a bad way to explain that you should expect that a good salad is going to take time and attention. I still use olive oil and red wine vinegar, but not exclusively. I've learned that although it is often safe to estimate a 2:1 ratio of oil to vinegar, it's best not to think of the proportion as a recipe. Instead, let taste lead the way, making sure the distinct flavor of each leaf is enhanced and never masked.

Peach Tart

Makes 1 (10-inch) tart

Most peaches grown on the island, ours included, are small, about the size of apricots or plums. At their peak they are delicious eaten in hand. In September, as the season wanes, we grab peaches from the tree when they are still a bit hard — but perfect for baking — and make this homey looking freeform tart.

FOR THE DOUGH
¾ cup all-purpose flour

¼ cup whole wheat flour

¼ cup cornmeal

½ teaspoon sugar

½ teaspoon salt

½ cup (1 stick) cold butter, cut into pieces

About ¼ cup ice water

FOR THE FILLING
2 pounds slightly under-ripe peaches

3 tablespoons sugar

2 tablespoons tapioca flour

1 teaspoon apple cider vinegar

1 egg, beaten

2 tablespoons butter, cut into pieces

Make the dough. Combine the all-purpose and whole wheat flours in a bowl. Mix in the cornmeal, sugar, and salt. Using a pastry cutter (or your fingers), work in the butter and just enough water so the dough can be formed into a ball. Wrap the dough in plastic wrap and refrigerate for at least 1 hour.

On a lightly floured surface, roll the dough out into a 14-inch round. Transfer the round to a lightly floured baking sheet and refrigerate for 15 minutes.

Heat the oven to 400°F.

Make the filling. Peel and pit the peaches, then cut them into wedges. Put the peaches in a bowl and add the sugar, tapioca flour, and vinegar. Mix well and set aside to macerate for about 10 minutes.

Spoon the peach mixture into the center of the chilled dough round. Fold the dough up over the filling, creating an overlapping edge about 2 inches wide. Pinch and crimp the edges around the filling, and then brush the exposed crust with beaten egg. Dot the filling with the butter, then bake until the crust begins to color, 10 to 15 minutes. Reduce the heat to 325°F and bake until the crust is golden and the filling is bubbly, about 30 minutes longer. Allow the tart to cool, then slice and serve.

MENU

bonito crudo

tautog soup

*beet & green
tomato salad*

bluefish
in parchment

crispy *potatoes*
& *aioli*

yogurt granita
with plums & tuile

◄9 / 25◄

LARSEN'S FISH MARKET

You don't want that," Betsy Larsen directs, noticing the spot in her fish case where my eyes have settled. Betsy knows me well, so I move on without hesitation, resuming my search for something to serve raw. She wraps a glistening fillet of bass for her only other early morning customer, then offers me her full attention, proposing several choices — September is a great fishing month in New England — and 20 minutes later I'm headed home with a whole bonito so bright-eyed and firm it needs no accompaniment beyond a slick of olive oil and a bit of fennel blossom.

Larsen's Fish Market is in Menemsha, the last commercial fishing harbor on Martha's Vineyard. It is halfway down the only street in this postcard-pretty village. Betsy is the boss. She is not physically imposing. Slight, five feet, six inches at best (though her oversized rubber boots add a little), she works tirelessly during the season. She starts her cleaning and inventory at dawn, hours before the store opens, and keeps working until well after the last customers have been served. As far as I can tell, she smiles the whole time.

Betsy is as good-natured as they come, but she is not someone I'd mess with. She got her grit from her father, Big Louie, a hulking man with hands that would swallow yours in a handshake. The men of his family fished in Norway and they kept at it after they left Europe in the twenties and settled on the Vineyard. He said over the years that it was hard for them here when they first arrived. It was difficult to fit into this tight-knit community with relationships interlaced for generations that reached back centuries. But the Larsens were good, hardworking people. Louie and his wife, Mary, lived on Beetlebung Corner across from the farm, and because my grandparents were also transplants (they'd moved to Chilmark from down-island), they all became fast friends.

Big Louie fished and fished well, but in 1969 he decided to try to make a different life for himself and his family and he opened a market. He fitted out the shack where Larsen's Fish Market still sits, perched on the sea wall, one door opening onto the street, the other onto the docks. Louie reared all his brood in and around the operation. Two of his sons now run fish shops down-island, and his nephew Stanley operates the only other fish market in Menemsha.

Big Louie used to tell people Betsy started working when she was fourteen. My guess is she started younger, but whenever she began, she picked up on things

quickly. In the end, Louie found his slender, genial daughter best suited of all of his children to the rigors of protecting the business he had worked so hard to build. Betsy's shop is sparkling and her fish, fresher than anyone else's. Walk through the door and you'll notice what you *don't* smell — there is not a whiff of fishiness in the air.

Betsy receives catch all day through her dock-side door. She handles each species with particularity — her bluefish differently than fluke and sole, or bonito, or mako, or swordfish (some of it still harpooned). She keeps her fish whole, buried in ice in the walk-in, and limits the display case to a few fillets, cutting more of what she needs as she goes, always rinsing with seawater as she works, which tightens the flesh ever so slightly. Everything is clean and everything is cold.

And Betsy beams as she waits on friends, locals, summer people, and first-timers, all with amiable efficiency. She is in constant motion in front of the lobster tanks, all fed by hoses pumping salt water from the ocean below. She is always pleasant and always in control of her shop. She keeps her knives sharpened and her floor clean, and provides the best fish you can get if you haven't caught it yourself.

Bonito Crudo

Serves 4

Atlantic bonito is a mid-sized, muscular, moderately fatty fish related to tuna and mackerel. Long popular in Spain and Italy, bonito has been ignored by cooks here for too long. If you get hold of a really fresh one, eat it raw. I like the bright pop that fennel blossoms bring with them. If you can't find blossoms, the crudo is nice as is or garnished with a soft herb like basil or mint.

> 8 ounces loin of freshly caught bonito
>
> About 1 teaspoon minced fennel blossoms
>
> About 1 teaspoon extra-virgin olive oil
>
> Sea salt

Handling the fish as little as possible and using a very sharp knife, remove the bloodline from the loin and cut away any discolored sections. Using a wet kitchen towel to wipe your knife as you go, slice the pieces of bonito about ¼ inch thick, so you have some texture in each bite, always cutting against the grain. It is easiest to do this with the skin still on (just as smoked salmon is sliced). Serve the bonito topped with a little minced fennel blossom, a few drops of olive oil, and a sprinkle of salt.

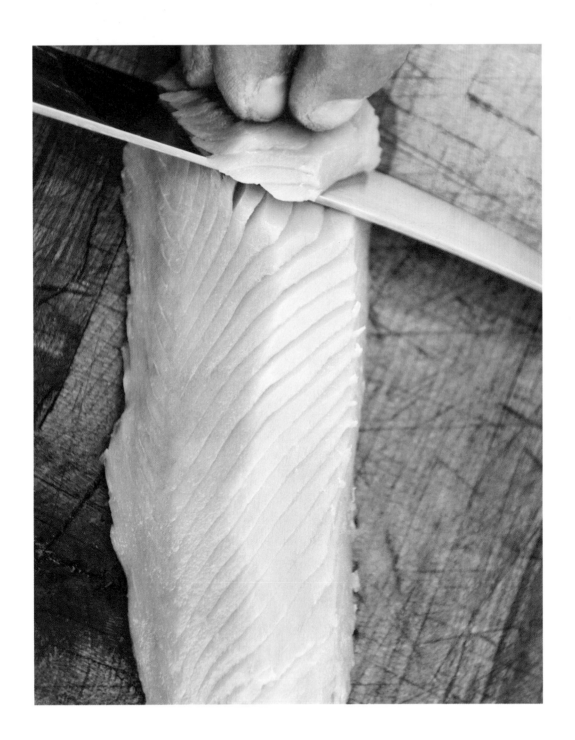

BLOSSOMS AND SEEDS

When you buy vegetables in the grocery store, you are almost never offered the whole plant. Fennel bulbs will be stacked in the produce section—trimmed for sale, the roots cut off, the dirty and discolored outer "leaves" of the bulb peeled away, and the fronds cut back. Even when several parts of a plant are for sale you may find them in entirely different parts of the store—fennel seeds will be in the spice aisle along with the coriander seeds, although you'll see fresh bunches of the herb (often labeled cilantro) in the produce section. But no matter where you look, you are unlikely to find any blossoms. It's too bad, because fennel and coriander blossoms are a wonderful way to flavor food, as are basil, chive, chervil, fava, and sweet pea blossoms. Blossoms have a tasty concentration of a plant's essence that is unexpected and nicely intense.

The best way to get your hands on blossoms is to grow your own. You can do this in a pot on the windowsill if you don't have a garden. Grow herbs and you will get the added bonus of access to your own fresh seeds—another ingredient I love. Fresh seeds zing and wake up a dish. I prefer to use *fresh* coriander seeds to make Crack Rice (page 119). You can substitute a combination of dried seeds and fresh leaves, but it isn't quite the same.

To collect herb seeds, simply let the plant blossom, then wilt. Snip the spent blossoms and gently remove the seeds. Save them in a closed container—I keep mine in the refrigerator—for as long as they keep their bright flavor.

Tautog Soup

Tautog (also known as blackfish) have a delicate rose-colored flesh that tastes rich and a little sweet—like the crabs, clams, and mussels they feed on. I make my stock with tautog bones, and these unexpectedly complex flavors emerge and harmonize. In fact the stock is so good it can stand on its own—like consommé. Off the island I have found tautog in Chinese fish markets—always a good source for less popular varieties of fish.

1 small tautog, about 2½ pounds, skinned and filleted, bones and
   head reserved, gills removed
3 tablespoons neutral oil, such as canola
2 small onions, halved and thinly sliced
Kosher salt
About 3 tablespoons basil blossoms (or torn basil leaves to taste)

Make the stock. Rinse the bones and head of the fish well under cold water and put in a large pot. Cover with water, about 1 gallon. Cover the pot and bring the water to a boil over high heat. Uncover and cook at a low rolling boil until the stock begins to cloud, about 45 minutes. Allow it to cool and settle for 15 minutes. Skim any scum from the surface, then ladle the stock into a clean container leaving the bones and sediment in the pot to be discarded. Season lightly with salt and refrigerate until you are ready to finish the soup.

Shortly before you plan to serve, cut the fish fillets into bite-sized pieces. Heat the oil in a high-sided skillet or Dutch oven over medium-low heat. Add the onions and sweat, cooking until they are soft and translucent but not yet beginning to color, 10 to 15 minutes.

Add the stock to the pan and bring it to a gentle simmer. Season the fish lightly with salt. Add to the stock and simmer until the tautog is just cooked through—opaque and tender—2 minutes or so. Taste the soup and adjust the seasoning with salt, then ladle into warm bowls. Put basil blossoms in each and serve.

Beet Salad with Green Tomatoes and Radishes

Serves 4

In October, beets are delicious, as sweet as they are in the spring; it's the cold that increases development of their sugar content. But chilly weather is hard on more delicate tomatoes. Frost forces farmers to think of uses for the green fruit that will never ripen on the vine. Not a problem: Sweet beets and tart green tomatoes are the perfect pair.

> 1 pound beets, scrubbed
>
> Kosher salt
>
> ¼ cup loosely packed parsley leaves
>
> 1 tablespoon red wine vinegar
>
> 1 tablespoon Champagne vinegar
>
> 1 tablespoon cider vinegar
>
> 2 tablespoons extra-virgin olive oil
>
> 1 large green tomato
>
> ⅓ cup roughly chopped radishes (2 to 3 radishes, depending on the size)

Put the beets in a pot and cover with water. Season the water with salt and bring to a boil over high heat. Cook the beets until they are easily pierced with a knife, 15 to 25 minutes. Drain and reserve.

Make the parsley puree. Fill a small pot with water and bring to a boil over high heat. Blanch the parsley until it is bright green, about 30 seconds. Drain the parsley and refresh in cold water. Puree in a blender with about 3 tablespoons water and reserve.

When the beets are cool enough to handle, peel them and then break each into 4 or so manageable pieces (you can cut them, but I like the way they look when they are torn). Put the beets in a bowl and dress them with the red wine, Champagne, and cider vinegars, and 1 tablespoon of oil. Season with salt and set aside to marinate.

Meanwhile, refill the pot and bring the water to a boil. Blanch the tomato to loosen the skin, 15 to 30 seconds. Drain the tomato, peel, then dice. Combine the tomato with the radishes in a bowl and dress with the remaining tablespoon of olive oil and several tablespoons of parsley puree (reserve any extra puree to stir into soups or stews). Season to taste with salt. Arrange the beets on plates, spoon the tomato mixture over them, and serve.

Bluefish in Parchment

Serves 4

I cook fish in parchment because it roasts while poaching in its own juices. You could leave the fish whole, but I butterfly and bone it, because it is easier to eat. Cooking in parchment is a great way to handle virtually any fish; of course, the cooking time will differ depending on the size and shape of the fish.

1 bluefish, about 3 pounds, scaled, gutted, and butterflied (ask your
 fish monger to do this or see Note on page 30)
About 3 tablespoons neutral oil, such as canola
Kosher salt
2 bunches dill, roughly chopped
1 lemon, thinly sliced
Aioli (page 34)

Heat the oven to 425°F. Rub the fish with a little oil, then sprinkle generously with salt. Place a large piece of parchment paper (16 by 24 inches) on a large baking sheet. Rub or brush a little more oil over the surface of the parchment, then arrange the dill, followed by the lemon slices, more or less evenly, over the surface. Lay the fish, flesh-side down, on the lemon and herbs. Rub or brush another piece of parchment with oil and place it oiled-side down on the fish (the oil both keeps the skin from sticking and conducts the heat).

To seal the parchment, carefully fold the edges tightly or, if you have a stapler handy, you can just fold each side over itself a couple of times and then staple the sheets together at regular intervals—the object is to keep all the juices locked into the parchment packet.

Roast the fish on the baking sheet on the middle rack of the oven for 8 minutes, then rotate the baking sheet 180 degrees so the fish cooks evenly. Roast until the oil in the packet is sizzling vigorously, smells toasty, and the fish feels "cooked"—still tender but not soft—when you press it through the parchment, about 3 minutes more. Allow the fish to rest for 5 minutes in the packet.

To serve, carefully slide the fish in the parchment onto a platter. Slit open the parchment, cutting away some or all of the paper (how much is an aesthetic choice), but trying to keep all the juices. Serve the aioli on the side.

Note: To butterfly a bluefish: Use a very sharp, flexible knife to make an incision in the belly, then cut upwards following the rib cage. Trace along the spine with your knife, cutting the flesh away from the bones as you move toward the tail. Repeat on the other side, freeing both fillets from their frame and allowing the fish to lie flat. Using sharp kitchen shears, make a cut through the spine at the tail of the fish and through the neck bones above the ribs. Peel the spine and ribs from the skin down the center of the fish, trimming bits that cling on with a sharp knife as you go. Remove the gills using scissors. Rinse the butterflied fish with cold salt water.

THE DERBY

She got her first glimpse and was frightened; the fish she had fought to bring in was shockingly large. It didn't look anything like a bass—way too big. She had struggled in the rain, her rod doubled, her line threatening to snap until she finally got it in the boat. It was enormous, its mouth broad enough to bring on nightmares. Molly, my sister, was twelve years old and she'd landed a fifty-pound striper.

Afterward, soaked and fatigued, she got an ice cream cone. That's what she wanted and had more than earned by reeling in the gigantic creature and then dragging it to the Derby headquarters to be weighed-in, declining the help my father offered. Molly won the Derby that year and became the youngest ever to do so—she still is.

My father started her while she was still in diapers. He taught her to cast and about the ways of the mighty bass and hungry blues. She absorbed it all and has always caught more than anyone, even him. She sings as she fishes (he didn't teach her to do that) and lures them to her by freeing her mind, eyes shut, until she feels them. He did teach her to read the ocean's tides, ripples, and shadows and the trails of sea birds, and to smell the wind and the weather. They have both always seemed to know when to pull hard and when to give.

In the early days of the Bass Derby the champions won a tract of land on the tip of the island, but by the time Molly won, the prize had become a chance to choose a key. If the key unlocked a padlock you'd win a boat or a truck. In the end Molly left boatless and truckless, because the key they gave her wasn't the right one. It was all right though, she wasn't old enough to drive anyway, and the story, the fishing, and the ice cream cone were enough for her.

Pan-Roasted Striped Bass

Serves 4

Skin-on striped bass fillets need to be cooked slowly so the heat penetrates the meaty fish. Watch the flame, take your time, and once the fillets are done—opaque and warm throughout—rest them for 5 minutes in the warm skillet. Striper skin is incredible, so I generally leave it on, but when that isn't my plan I crisp it separately to serve as a garnish: Lay the skin between lightly greased sheets of parchment paper on a baking sheet and then toast it in a low oven for about half an hour.

> 1½ pounds skin-on striped bass fillet, cut into 4 (6-ounce) portions
> Kosher salt
> About 3 tablespoons extra-virgin olive oil

Heat a large skillet over high heat. Season the fish on both sides with salt, going a little heavier on the skin side. Add a good coating of oil to the pan. When the oil is hot, put the fish in the pan, skin-side down, and reduce the heat to medium. Cook over medium heat until the skin begins to firm, about 1 minute more, then reduce the heat further to medium-low (you want to hear a nice, gentle sizzle). Baste with the pan juices and cook until the skin is brown and the fish is opaque halfway up the sides, about 8 minutes. Now turn the fillets on their edges, let them cook a minute or so on each, then flip to the flesh side to finish, about 1 minute more. Turn off the flame and allow the fillets to rest, then serve.

Potatoes Crisped in Olive Oil

Serves 4

My favorite way to serve these potatoes, as addictive as French fries but much easier to make, is with both aioli *and* romesco sauce, but they are also wonderful as is.

> 1 pound small Yukon gold potatoes, scrubbed
>
> Kosher salt
>
> About 2 tablespoons extra-virgin olive oil
>
> About 1 tablespoon celery leaves (or tender innermost stalks chopped small)
>
> ¼ cup Aioli (next page)
>
> ¼ cup Romesco Sauce (page 10)

Put the potatoes in a pot and cover with water. Add salt and bring to a boil over high heat. Reduce the flame and simmer until the potatoes are tender, 20 minutes; drain.

Heat a large skillet over medium-high heat. Add enough oil to coat the pan well, then add the potatoes. Smash them with a spatula—you want to increase the area in contact with the heat (it is OK if some potatoes merge and OK if they remain separate). Season them lightly with salt and fry, shaking the pan occasionally, until they are brown and crisp on the bottom, about 10 minutes. Flip the potatoes and continue cooking until both sides are golden, about 10 minutes more. Toss the potatoes with the celery leaves, add salt to taste, and serve with aioli and romesco sauce on the side.

Aioli

Makes about ¾ cup

The trick to making a successful aioli (essentially garlic mayonnaise) is adding the olive oil to the egg at a much slower pour than you think you should. If you are making a large batch (it will keep for about a week refrigerated in an airtight container) you can use a food processor, otherwise doing it by hand is the way to go.

½ small clove garlic

About ¼ teaspoon salt

Pinch of minced lemon zest

2 egg yolks

1 tablespoon freshly squeezed lemon juice

½ to ¾ cup extra-virgin olive oil

Mince the garlic with the salt, chopping it until it is a paste. Transfer the paste to a bowl and add the lemon zest and egg yolks. Whisk together. Add the lemon juice and, whisking constantly, very gradually add the oil in a slow stream. If you plan to use your aioli as a sauce or base to a dressing, stop adding oil when it is the consistency of thin pancake batter. If you want it thicker, continue adding oil. Use the aioli immediately or store covered in the refrigerator.

Yogurt Granita

Serves 4

You don't need any special equipment to make granita — essentially Italian ice. The only thing to keep in mind is that you need to stir the granita from time to time so it doesn't freeze solid.

    2 cups plain yogurt
    1 tablespoon sugar

Combine the yogurt and sugar in a shallow container. Freeze until the granita begins to solidify, about 20 minutes. Stir and return the granita to the freezer. Mix every 20 minutes, breaking up any clumps of ice, until the granita is frozen but frothy, about 1 hour, then serve.

Roasted Plums

Serves 4

Black peppercorns intensify the spicy notes in the red wine, which balances the sugar in the plums.

    4 medium plums, seeded and quartered
    ½ teaspoon black peppercorns
    About 1 cup dry red wine
    1 tablespoon sugar

Heat the oven to 450°F. Put the plums in a baking dish large enough to hold them in a snug single layer. Add the peppercorns and enough wine to cover, then sprinkle with the sugar. Roast, basting the plums regularly until they soften, about 45 minutes. Cool thoroughly, then strain the pan sauce, reducing it so it is nicely syrupy. Serve over the plums.

Oat Tuiles

Makes about 30 cookies

Wonderful on their own or as an accompaniment to granita, these cookies are also good crumbled over Maple Crème Fraîche Ice Cream (page 160).

  5 tablespoons butter

  2 tablespoons sugar

  1 tablespoon honey

  ½ cup oats

  4 teaspoons whole wheat flour

Combine the butter, sugar, and honey in a small saucepan and melt over medium-low heat. Remove the pan from the heat and stir in the oats and then the flour. Allow the batter to cool completely.

Heat the oven to 325°F. Working in batches, drop small dollops (about ½ teaspoon each) about 4 inches apart on an ungreased baking sheet. Bake the cookies until they are golden, 4 to 6 minutes. Cool and serve.

october dinner

veal tartar
egg yolk and shiitake

cauliflower salad

lobster pan roast
tomato butter and toast

walnut pear cake

LOBSTERS

He worked on commercial trawlers and longliners when he came home from the army, but my father has always preferred to trap lobsters and fish for the joy of a day on the water and the reward of a fresh-caught meal. When I was growing up he had a recreational permit that allowed him ten pots. We sank them in Menemsha Pond as early as we could each spring.

Our mooring was at the mouth of Herring Creek. "The crick," as we called it, was the route herring took (once in large numbers) from the brackish waters of Squibnocket Pond, where they'd spawned, out to Menemsha Pond, and finally to the sea. There's a large rock on the shore there. That's where my brother and I perched when we were young to watch Dad get things ready on lobstering days.

He'd pull the dinghy from high above the tide line, slip the oarlocks from his pocket (he kept them at home to forestall thieves), set the oars, and load the boat. Then he'd row out smoothly and powerfully to get things squared away on the boat — a twenty-five-foot Seacraft. We'd wait impatiently until he puttered in close to shore. Then he'd wave and cut the engine, our signal to plunge in and race to the boat, each anxious to be the first to reach up an arm and be yanked aboard.

Opening up the engine, he'd take us for a spin, breaking the glassy surface of the water as we circled the pond before he set us to work hauling pots. I remember looking up at him standing tall, six-foot-two (then as now), his mustache flattened by the wind, tinted glasses protecting his eyes. He'd toss his worn baseball cap onto the center console as I squinted away tears, my eyes stung by the spray.

In the winter, when work slowed down, my dad would paint his buoys blue. Snagging those buoys was our job from the start, even when the traps still outweighed us. He would pull the boat up as close as he could and idle the engine. My brother and I would hang over the side, legs sticking straight up in the air, struggling to grab the buoy's wooden pegs. My father would look on ready to grasp the waist of whichever boy seemed likely to topple.

Once one of us got hold, he would take over, effortlessly hoisting the pot up and out of the water. Then he'd set us to prying the lobsters from the traps. They'd cling hard to the cage, then viciously snap and flail, sensing their last shot at freedom. Going lobster by lobster, we'd pull them out, trying not to leave their claws behind, always working to keep our fingers safe and whole, as we anchored

my father's beat-up metal gauge in their eye sockets to measure them. We tossed the small ones back into the water like Frisbees and then we'd band the rest, stilling their snapping weapons with my father's plier-like tool long enough to bind them with thick rubber bands.

We replaced the empty bait bags with full containers of rotted salted fish scooped from our bait barrels — sturdy fifty-five-gallon containers with large plastic lids we kept stocked next to our barn. Pots emptied and bait refreshed, we'd drop the traps back overboard, careful of the retreating rope at our feet. My father told us he'd once gotten caught and dragged overboard when he was working on a swordfishing longliner. He only survived by cutting himself free as he was dragged deep. The frightening image gripped us fully and did its job. We kept as far from the strangling cord as we could.

We lined our pots through the pond, except in years when the spider crabs beat out the lobsters for that choice real estate. In those years, we would motor out and sink traps in Vineyard Sound along the north shore. Either way we usually wound up bobbing and drifting with the tide, a safe distance from the craggy coastline, trying to catch black sea bass and bluefish. We'd catch our fill and head back to feast — throughout the summer and then one last time in October.

Veal Tartare with Shiitakes

Serves 4

When you serve food raw it is especially important to know where it comes from. I get most of my veal from a dairy farm, Mermaid Farm, a wonderful operation run by Allen Healy and Caitlin Jones. They cull male calves to save grass and hay for their cows. The meat from their young pasture-raised animals is pink, gamey, and lean—very different from, and much more delicious than, traditional milk-raised veal.

> ½ pound veal top round or eye round from a reliable source
>
> 1 tablespoon extra-virgin olive oil, plus a high-quality extra-virgin to finish
>
> 1 tablespoon fresh lemon juice
>
> Kosher salt
>
> Freshly ground black pepper
>
> 4 ounces shiitake mushrooms, stems removed
>
> 4 fresh egg yolks

Trim the veal, removing any fat, sinew, and silver skin (or ask your butcher to do it). Finely dice the veal—a sharp knife is essential here. I like to work 2 ounces at a time, keeping the rest of the meat chilled in a bowl set over ice. The meat can be diced several hours in advance.

Just before serving, dress the diced veal with the olive oil and lemon juice and season with salt and pepper to taste.

Slice the shiitakes paper-thin. Spoon the veal tartare onto plates, making a small well in the top of each mound. Arrange the shiitakes around the meat. Season the mushrooms with a little salt and pepper and a drizzle of olive oil. Settle an egg yolk atop each serving of veal, season with another sprinkling of salt, and serve.

Cauliflower, Chickpeas, and Green Olives

Serves 4

On Beetlebung, we harvest cauliflower very young, then use the whole plant. The tender stalks go into the dressing in this recipe. The leaves are also good from a young plant. Blanched and chopped, they can be tossed with the florets.

1 medium head cauliflower, trimmed, cored, and divided into
  florets, core reserved

¼ cup extra-virgin olive oil, plus a high-quality extra-virgin to
  finish

Kosher salt

2 tablespoons red wine vinegar

1 medium shallot, diced

Pinch crushed red pepper

2 cups cooked chickpeas (see Dried Beans, next page)

10 green olives, pitted and roughly chopped

Freshly ground black pepper (optional)

Bring a large pot of salted water to a boil over high heat. Add the cauliflower core and cook until tender, about 5 minutes. Remove with a slotted spoon and reserve. Add the florets to the boiling water and cook until just tender, about 2 minutes. Drain, then refresh under cold water. Transfer the florets to a bowl, dress with 1 tablespoon of the olive oil, and season lightly with salt.

Make the "salsa blanca." Mince the blanched cauliflower core. Combine the vinegar, shallot, and crushed pepper in a medium bowl. Add the minced core and a generous pinch of salt. Mix in the remaining 3 tablespoons olive oil, the chickpeas, and olives.

Arrange the florets on plates. Spoon the "salsa blanca" over the cauliflower, drizzle with good extra-virgin olive oil, season with pepper, then serve.

DRIED BEANS

I like to buy dried beans from small producers. I find they taste better and cook more evenly. I try to buy beans that have not been on the shelf too long. Although they are dried they can become stale.

I cook most dried beans (including chickpeas and white beans) the same way. I soak them overnight in water to cover by a couple of inches. Some people assert that soaking isn't necessary, but I believe it helps the beans cook evenly. Then I drain the beans and put them in a pot with fresh water to cover by about 2 inches. Sometimes I add some aromatics—onion, celery, peppercorns, or a bay leaf—but mostly I don't, I want the beans to taste like beans.

I slowly bring them to a simmer over medium heat. Once the water comes up, I adjust the heat so it is just barely bubbling—beans like to be cooked slowly—and let them cook until they are tender. The time depends on the type of beans and their age. I don't like chewy beans, but I also don't want them mushy, so as soon as they are tender I pull the pot off the heat, season the beans with salt, and let them cool in the cooking liquid. Expect 1 cup of dried beans to yield about 3 cups cooked.

Home-cooked beans are much better than canned, but when time forces me, I will resort to the latter. When I do, I rinse them very thoroughly and dress them very carefully.

Lobster Pan-Roast with Tomato Butter Crostini

Serves 4

I don't need a party to eat lobster, but it's fun to make it an occasion. And while I still love a midsummer lobster dinner, my favorite time for lobster is the fall — it reminds me of the last catch just before we pulled up the pots. A lobster you take in the fall tastes a little more wild to me than the sweet, softer shelled summer lobsters. There is something particularly satisfying about eating your fill with close friends, on a cool night, using bread to mop up all the butter and juices, not caring if it is all a bit messy.

2 small lobsters, each about 1¼ pounds, females if available

Kosher salt

¼ cup tomato paste

3 tablespoons sherry vinegar

¾ cup (1½ sticks) butter, softened

2 teaspoons chopped fresh marjoram

2 lemons

1 small baguette, split lengthwise; or 1 loaf country bread, thickly sliced; toasted or grilled

Bring a large pot of salted water to a boil and organize an ice bath. Separate the tails and claws from the lobsters' bodies. Blanch the tails and claws for 5 minutes, then drain and put them into the ice bath to stop the cooking. Crack the shells and remove the meat. (This can be done several hours ahead; refrigerate until you are ready to make the pan-roast.)

Meanwhile, retrieve the roe (if there is any) from the bodies of the females by pulling out the dark green sack. Put the roe sacks in a small container and refrigerate. Freeze the lobster bodies to use for another purpose.

Combine the tomato paste and vinegar in a small pan and reduce over medium-high heat, stirring occasionally, until you are left with about 2 tablespoons of tomato concentrate. Allow the tomato to cool, then stir it into ½ cup of the softened butter. Add the marjoram, then season with salt and the juice from half a lemon. Taste the butter and adjust the seasoning if necessary with more salt and lemon juice. Pack the butter into ramekins, cover, and refrigerate.

Squeeze the roe, if you have it, from the sacks into a small bowl. Remove and discard the vein that runs down the back of the lobster tails and then cut the tails into ½-inch pieces. Tear the claws into pieces about the same size. Pull the tomato butter from the refrigerator.

Melt the remaining 4 tablespoons butter over very low heat in a skillet or flameproof serving dish large enough to hold all the lobster. Cut a lemon in quarters, squeeze the juice into the pan, and add the rinds. (If you want to, you can add a tablespoon of water—this helps to keep the butter from "breaking.")

Season the lobster and pan sauce lightly with salt. Add the lobster and roe to the pan and warm, basting with the butter mixture, until the lobster is heated through and the roe turns bright red. Remove the lemon rinds.

Serve the lobster with the toasted bread and tomato butter—spread it ahead, or do as I do and just let everyone dig in as they will. (Save any extra tomato butter—it is great on sandwiches.)

Variation: Lobster with Spaetzle

I love lobster and pasta: store-bought linguine, homemade cavatelli, or easy-to-make spaetzle—free-form pasta popular in Switzerland, Austria, and Germany. Follow the recipe above, par-cooking the lobster, removing the meat from the shell, and making the tomato butter. Then make spaetzle batter by combining 2 cups flour and 1 teaspoon salt with 2 beaten eggs and 1 cup water. Mix everything together, then let the batter rest at room temperature for 1 hour.

Set a colander over a pot of boiling salted water. Working in batches, force the batter through the colander into the boiling water. Cook the spaetzle until they float, about 3 minutes, then transfer to an oiled baking sheet to cool. Dress the cooled spaetzle with a little olive oil.

Heat a generous skim of olive oil in a large skillet over high heat. When it is hot, add several tablespoons of spaetzle. Working in batches, toast the spaetzle, tossing them in the oil until they are golden brown, then transfer to a bowl. When all the spaetzle are toasted, wipe out the skillet and add the lobster, a dollop of tomato butter, and some roe (if there is any), then season with salt and lemon juice. Add the toasted spaetzle and cook together until the lobster is heated through. Add some chopped basil or fennel blossoms and serve.

Pear Walnut Cake

Makes 1 (9-inch) cake

This caramelized upside-down cake is a versatile recipe. I use pears here, but apples are also a good option.

FOR THE CARAMEL

5 tablespoons butter

¾ cup sugar

FOR THE CAKE

½ cup (1 stick) butter

1 cup shelled walnuts

1 cup sugar

¼ cup all-purpose flour

¼ cup whole wheat flour

Pinch salt

6 Seckel pears (or 4 Asian pears), peeled, cored, and sliced ¼ inch thick

¾ cup egg whites (about 6 eggs), at room temperature

Make the caramel. Line the bottom of a 9-inch springform pan with parchment. Melt the butter with the sugar in a saucepan over medium heat, stirring occasionally. As the caramel begins to color, stir it more frequently. Cook, reducing the heat if necessary to prevent the caramel from bubbling over, until it is deep amber, about 3 minutes. Pour the caramel into the prepared pan and let cool.

Make the cake. Heat the oven to 325°F. Brown the butter in a small saucepan over medium heat, stirring frequently. Remove from the heat and reserve. Combine the walnuts and ½ cup of the sugar in a food processor and grind to a coarse meal; reserve. Whisk the all-purpose flour with the whole wheat flour and salt in a large bowl. Stir in the walnut mixture.

Arrange the pear slices in a single overlapping layer on the caramel in the pan. Beat the egg whites in a bowl or mixer until frothy. Gradually whisk in the remaining ½ cup sugar, then whip the whites to shiny peaks. Fold half of the flour mixture into the egg whites, then fold in half of the browned butter, then repeat.

Spoon the batter over the pears, spreading it evenly. Set the cake on a baking sheet and bake until golden and fluffy and a toothpick inserted in the center comes out clean, about 45 minutes. Let the cake cool for 5 minutes, then take it out of the pan, flip it over, and cool it completely. Slice and serve.

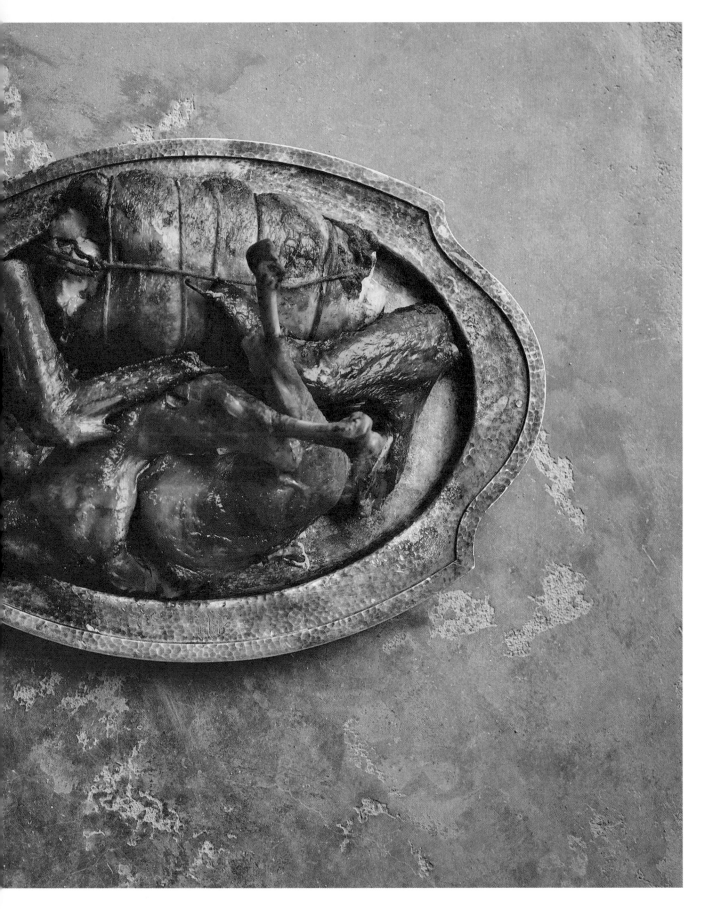

LATE HARVEST

NOVEMBER

VENISON ON CEDAR

FROMAGE BLANC CROSTINO
WITH HONEY, CHILI, & CHARD

RABBIT & FENNEL

CARROTS & CELERY ROOT

BEET CAKE
WITH FENNEL ICING

GROWING UP HUNTING

Knowing how to find, kill, and prepare what you eat are primal skills. I learned as I grew up. Stalking an animal well is something you are shown by someone who was shown before you. Skinning, dressing, hanging, and boning are only mastered by doing. I am drawn to the practice and to the equipment of hunting. In families like ours, guns are handed down or thoughtfully gifted as you grow up. Hunting knives, you learn, are tools that must be kept sharp and wielded artfully. Eating what you kill is a shared pleasure. The deer, rabbit, duck, squirrels, and birds we hunt here are delicacies. They eat a diet they choose, and are constantly moving, flying, and burrowing to survive, which makes their meat both tasty and healthful.

When I was young my father's double-barreled shotgun hung from a beam in our living room. He kept his other guns in the closet (along with his old army uniform). He started teaching us, first my older brother, then me, to shoot when we were little. He began by having us hit targets, scavenged soda and beer bottles, on the winter dunes at Long Beach. We used a .22 he kept to dispatch rats and skunks. A .22 doesn't have much kick. We moved next to bottles tossed into Squibnocket Pond, then graduated to mourning doves, then to rabbits and squirrels. Rabbits were abundant and easy to get. Squirrels were more nimble, but in my opinion (then and now) even more tasty.

When my brother was twelve he was given a shotgun for Christmas. A shotgun is sufficient firepower to take on ducks, geese, and deer. It is a powerful gun and the gift signaled that my brother was entering adulthood. I was two years younger and my dad didn't think I was ready — he was right, but that didn't stop me. I "borrowed" and learned to shoot my brother's gift. I can still feel the ache in my shoulder that came as I tried to cradle the blow after discharge, and can still hear the pop, inches from my ear, that left a ringing in its wake.

My dad prefers to hunt by himself. He grows his "hunting beard" when deer season starts, the first scruff appearing when bow-and-arrow season opens, before Thanksgiving. He maintains it through shotgun season, and then by muzzle-loading season he has a fully realized beard. He walks the woods a lot in these late-fall and early-winter months looking for "ruts," spots where bucks have rubbed their scent onto trees to attract females. My father is a skillful, confident hunter and a sure shot, and when the time comes he is able to be choosy about which animal he takes down. He prefers young deer, knowing their meat will be mild and tender, but he will also take a healthy mature doe.

When I was growing up, he would leave the house before first light. After taking down a deer, he would eviscerate it, then haul it home and hang it from the rafters of our barn. The walls were covered with antlers, reminders of earlier seasons, the racks all splattered with the droppings of generations of swallows who nested among the pronged "branches." Deer would hang throughout the season, waiting to be skinned and broken down for the freezer. Some of the meat would be ground for burgers (a little dry), and some made into sausage by my father's buddy Babe, a butcher on the mainland (spicy and speckled with pork fat), then it would all go into the freezer with the prized grill-worthy cuts (including the boned-out legs and loins) and the rest labeled simply "stew."

The "backstrap" (the tenderloin), the very best cut, was always long gone by the time the rest of the meat found its way to the freezer. My father cut the backstrap off when he got an animal home and hung. And he'd cook it as soon as he washed up. It didn't matter what time it was, it wasn't a meal but rather a treat and a tribute. We'd all eat the rare slices of juicy meat eagerly, standing together, skewering bites from a shared plate, mopping up any juices, appreciating every savored mouthful.

Venison Loin in Cedar

Serves 4

Venison loin is a delicacy. The meat is tender and succulent; it tastes of the acorns and viburnum leaves the animals feed on. Cedar goes well with venison. It has a wonderful mentholated flavor, similar to rosemary but even more lively. Luckily I have a tree growing right outside my kitchen, so I can easily snip off young pale green boughs.

About 1½ pounds venison loin (or venison backstrap)

Kosher salt

2 handfuls cedar sprigs (or 6 sprigs rosemary)

¾ cup plus 2 tablespoons neutral oil, such as canola

About 1 teaspoon sherry vinegar

Freshly ground black pepper

A day before you plan to cook, rub the venison with a liberal amount of salt. Wrap it in the cedar sprigs, then in plastic wrap, and refrigerate overnight.

About 45 minutes before you plan to serve, remove the venison from the refrigerator and allow it to come to room temperature. Meanwhile, combine ¾ cup oil and the vinegar in a saucepan. Add a big sprig of the cedar (take one from the venison wrap) and place the saucepan on a back burner, off the heat, to let the cedar and oil get to know one another.

Heat the remaining 2 tablespoons oil in a large skillet over medium-high heat. Add the venison and cook, browning it on all sides and basting with the pan juices, until rare to medium-rare, about 10 minutes for the loin (or about 2 minutes per side for the backstrap). Remove the venison from the heat, pour the cedar-infused oil over the meat, and set aside to rest for 5 minutes, turning it several times so it marinates evenly.

Remove the venison from the marinade. Cut it into slices about ½ inch thick, crack fresh pepper over the top, and serve.

Fromage Blanc Crostini with Honey and Chard

Serves 4

I get fromage blanc from Mermaid Farm — it is creamy and wonderful and charmingly never quite the same. Vermont Creamery also makes a nice fromage blanc, or you can substitute fresh ricotta — either homemade (see the Cheese Blintzes recipe, page 202) or store-bought.

> 1 small bunch chard (8 to 10 stalks), stems removed and reserved for another purpose
>
> Kosher salt
>
> ½ baguette, cut into 4 pieces (split the baguette in half lengthwise, then cut each half in half again) and lightly toasted
>
> About 2 teaspoons honey
>
> About ½ cup fromage blanc
>
> Crushed red pepper
>
> 1 lemon, halved
>
> Freshly ground black pepper

Blanch the chard leaves in salted boiling water until tender, about 5 minutes. Drain and refresh in cold water. Remove from the water, squeezing out the excess, then roughly chop.

Drizzle each piece of baguette with honey and then spread with cheese. Season the cheese with salt and crushed pepper. Put chard on the toasted bread, give each a squeeze of lemon juice and a few grinds of black pepper, and serve.

Rabbit with Fennel

Serves 4

I make a "reinforced stock" by adding rabbit bones to chicken stock for extra flavor, then add anchovies to the aromatics (onions and fennel) to bring a slightly briny complexity to the rabbit's braising liquid. I like to cook the legs gently for a good while, but hold off on the stuffed loins, finishing them just before serving so they stay juicy.

> 1 rabbit, about 3½ pounds, cut into 6 pieces: the front and back legs, the saddle deboned and cut into the two loins with the bellies attached (have your butcher do this or try it yourself); reserve the saddle bones, liver, and heart
>
> About 6 tablespoons neutral oil, such as canola
>
> 2 cups chicken stock, preferably homemade (see page 140)
>
> Kosher salt
>
> 1 medium yellow onion, cut into thin wedges
>
> 2 small to medium fennel bulbs, trimmed and thinly sliced (reserve the trimmings to make Carrots and Celery Root Cooked in Fennel Broth, page 64)
>
> 2 cloves garlic, 1 sliced, 1 minced
>
> 4 anchovy fillets packed in olive oil
>
> ½ cup dry white wine
>
> ¼ cup loosely packed parsley leaves, minced
>
> ¼ teaspoon minced lemon zest

Reinforce the stock. Brown the reserved rabbit bones in a skim of oil in a large pot over medium-high heat for about 15 minutes. Add the chicken stock, bring to a boil, then reduce the heat and simmer until the stock is reduced by a little less than half, about 25 minutes.

Prepare the liver and heart. Heat a skim of oil in a skillet over high heat. Add the liver and heart and sauté, cooking just until they are browned on both sides and nicely firm, about 2 minutes. Remove from the pan, cool, and reserve in the refrigerator.

Prepare the legs. Heat a large skillet over medium-high heat. Season the front and back legs of the rabbit liberally with salt. Add enough oil to cover the surface of the skillet, about 2 tablespoons. Working in batches if necessary to avoid crowding the pan, brown the legs on all sides, 15 to 20 minutes. Transfer the legs to a plate lined with paper towels to drain.

Add a little more oil to the pan if necessary, then add the onion, fennel, and sliced garlic. Cook over medium-high heat, stirring frequently, until the vegetables are nicely colored, about 15 minutes. Return the seared legs to the pan and add the anchovies. Shake and stir the pan to mix the contents, then add the wine. Bring the wine to a boil, turning the rabbit legs over once or twice as it reduces. When the pan is almost dry, about 5 minutes, strain the reinforced stock into it. Allow the stock to come to a boil, then reduce the heat. Partially cover the pan and gently simmer the rabbit, turning the pieces every 20 minutes or so, and adding ½ cup of water from time to time if the pan gets dry. Braise until the legs are tender, the meat pulls away from the bone, and the braising liquid has concentrated, about 1 hour and 15 minutes.

Stuff the rabbit loins while the legs are braising. Chop the liver and heart. Combine the chopped liver mixture with the minced garlic, parsley, and lemon zest. Season the loins lightly with salt and lay flat on a clean work surface, skinned-side down. Divide the liver stuffing between them, then roll up each and secure with kitchen string. Heat a small skillet over medium-high heat. Add a skim of oil and brown the rabbit loins on all sides, about 8 minutes.

Add the loins to the braising legs and finish cooking, basting them and turning them in the simmering sauce, about 5 minutes more. (You can check for doneness by inserting a metal skewer in the center of a loin; remove it and touch the edge to your lip—if it is hot the rabbit is done.) Cut away the strings and slice the loins. Arrange on a serving plate with the legs and pan sauce.

Carrots and Celery Root Cooked in Fennel Broth

Serves 4

Cooking carrots and celery root in a broth made from fennel trimmings adds freshness and complexity to a simple dish. Because the cooking times can vary considerably depending on the age of the vegetables and exactly how you cut them, I cook the carrots and celery root separately.

> Trimmings from 2 fennel bulbs (or 1 small fennel bulb, chopped)
> Kosher salt
> 2 medium celery roots, peeled and cut into pieces about 1 inch long
> 3 medium carrots, scrubbed and cut into pieces about 1 inch long

Put the fennel in a pot. Add 1 gallon water and bring to a boil over high heat. Lower the heat and vigorously simmer until the broth has reduced by half, about 15 minutes. Strain the broth and return to the pot.

Bring the broth back up to a boil, add the celery root, and cook until it is tender but has a bite at its center; check after 5 minutes, though it will likely take longer. Using a slotted spoon, transfer the celery root to a bowl, cover (to keep warm), and reserve. Add the carrots to the pot and cook them until they reach the same toothsome tenderness, checking after 5 minutes as well. Drain the carrots (reserving the broth — refrigerate or freeze it and use as you would vegetable stock). Combine the carrots with the celery root. Check for seasoning, adding salt if needed, and serve.

EMMA'S PEAR CIDER

Emma Young is drawn to traditional ways of doing things. She spends her days working in her studio on Lambert's Cove as a letterpress artist and she plants and tends her garden by hand. When we make cider we borrow her family's seventy-five-year-old cider press.

Asian pears are best for cider — they are crisp and dry and not too sweet. We like to include a few under-ripe pears to boost the tang. You'll need a full 5-gallon bucket of pears to make 3 wine bottles of cider.

Using the old press, line the barrel with cheesecloth and go pear by pear (there is no need to peel or wash the pears unless you are unsure of your source and fear exposure to pesticides), grinding the pears as you crank. When the bucket is filled with mash it is time to press. Tie up the cheesecloth before you begin pressing, and make sure to position a pot to capture the cider that flows.

Once the fruit is pressed the cider must be flash-pasteurized — you'll need a candy thermometer to test the temperature. Put the cider in a pot and heat it until it reaches 180°F. (That's what you need to kill bacteria, which is especially important if you have picked up any "drops" from the ground.)

Decant the hot cider into a sanitized carboy (a large sealable jug). Emma has a plastic carboy with a tight-fitting lid and an airlock. Allow the cider to cool to between 80°F and 90°F (measure with the candy thermometer), then add the yeast. Champagne yeast is best because it gives the cider a light effervescence. You can find it at homebrew stores or online in packets premeasured for 5 gallons. I don't add any sugar because the cider itself has enough naturally to create alcohol.

Place the sealed carboy in a warm, dark room for three days — giving the yeast plenty of time to have its way with the pear sugars. You'll get energetic air bubbles released through the airlock after a little while; they will become more intense and then subside some by the end of the third day.

At this point the cider is ready to bottle. Any sanitized glass bottle will do. Green wine or water bottles work perfectly and look beautiful. Seal each with a bottle capper and fresh cap. Then put the cider back in a warm, dark room to age for a month or six weeks — that is all you need. But be forewarned: an explosion or two is to be expected. And try a bottle before you offer it around — one of the beauties of cider is that every batch is unique — it is all a bit alive. The last batch we made got better and better, drier and drier, as we drank it through the winter.

Beet Cake with Fennel Icing

Makes 1 (9-inch) cake

This cake is moister and more delicious than carrot cake. Kids love it—although I've found it's sometimes best to let them taste it before telling them what's in it.

FOR THE CAKE

2 cups grated peeled beets (about 1 pound)

2 cups sugar

2½ cups all-purpose flour

2 teaspoons unsweetened cocoa powder

1 teaspoon baking soda

1 cup neutral oil, such as canola

1 cup yogurt

2 eggs, beaten

1 teaspoon white vinegar

¼ teaspoon vanilla extract

FOR THE BEET JAM

3 apples (any eating apple)

1 cup grated peeled beets (about ½ pound)

½ cup sugar

FOR THE FROSTING

1 cup milk

1½ teaspoons fennel seeds

3 tablespoons all-purpose flour

½ pound (2 sticks) butter, at room temperature

1 cup sugar

Make the cake. Combine the grated beets with ½ cup of the sugar in a large bowl. Mix and set aside until the mixture looks "juicy," about 40 minutes.

Heat the oven to 350°F. Grease a 9-inch springform pan. In a bowl, whisk the flour with the cocoa and baking soda.

Add the remaining 1½ cups of sugar to the beet mixture, then add the oil, yogurt, eggs, vinegar, and vanilla and mix well. Fold in the flour mixture. Spoon the batter into the prepared pan. Bake the cake until it bounces back when pressed; start checking after 1 hour, but it may take longer. Allow the cake to cool for 10 minutes, then remove it from the pan and allow it to cool completely.

Meanwhile, make the jam. Peel, core, and chop the apples. Put them in a saucepan with the grated beets and sugar. Cook over low heat, stirring occasionally and breaking up any chunks as you go, until the jam is very soft and spreadable, about 35 minutes. Allow it to cool.

Make the frosting while the cake bakes and the jam cooks. Combine the milk and fennel seeds in a saucepan and bring to a simmer over medium heat. Pull the pan off the stove, cover, and let the milk steep for an hour.

Strain the milk (discarding the fennel seeds) and return to the pan. Add the flour and whisk continuously over medium heat until the milk thickens, about 5 minutes (your whisk will begin to leave "tracks"). Pour the mixture into a bowl, cover with plastic wrap so it doesn't form a skin, and set aside to cool.

Using an electric mixer, beat the butter with the sugar until white and fluffy. With the mixer running, slowly add the fennel milk. Beat just until the frosting is light and airy.

Assemble the cake. When the cake is cool, cut it in half through the middle with a serrated knife, creating two more or less equal rounds. Carefully put the bottom round on a plate or cake stand. Spread the cut surface evenly with the beet jam, then lay the second round, cut-side down, on top. Frost the top and sides of the cake, slice, and serve.

a harvest m*ea*l

at

TEA LANE

FARM

FARMING FLOWERS

A lifetime ago Poppy saved his mother's dahlia bulbs. He used them to plant a garden for my grandmother when they first moved to Beetlebung Farm. He carefully dug them and stored them in the basement each winter, then replanted them every year of their lives together. Krishana Collins purchased half his bulbs when age finally caused him to limit his planting. She gave him a check for $274 and they were both delighted, she with her purchase and he with her. He flirted, as he did with everyone, but I was surprised to notice his teasings making my grandmother jealous — I'd never seen that before. But I suppose I understand.

Krishana grew up in Florida but settled on the Vineyard because she felt she had finally found her home, the community she needed to replace the loss she suffered when her mother died. I first saw her one spring at the farmers' market before her freckles were masked by a tan and the summer crowds filled the booths. She leaned languidly on a tent pole surrounded by tins of remarkable-looking flowers organized by color and type. The wind tossed her tousled, curly hair and the sun shimmered in her smudged glasses as she set to work, making bouquets with a mixture of wild and cultivated blossoms and sprigs, artfully managing to find the perfect balance between pretty and rough. She'd pass her handiwork to her customers, traces of pollen coloring her fingers.

She stopped by to help Poppy "split" the rest of his cache a few weeks after her big bulb purchase. They sat, hands working, hers small and deft, his gnarled and swollen but skilled. As they made their way through the work, Krishana leaned in, hoping to catch hold of some of his experience and wisdom.

I first won the chance to spend time with her by sinking fence posts until my hands were bloody and my back ached. I thought she would appreciate the fence and the effort, because like my grandfather, Krishana needs to farm. There is no other way for her in this life than to be a grower. Like Poppy, she was a farmer long before she owned an acre of land. She worked on rented land or for other people, whatever it took to follow her calling. Now she has her own place, a seventy-five-year lease on a farm owned by the Martha's Vineyard Land Bank Commission, a local conservation organization. It's a beautiful property set where Tea Lane meets Middle Road. Her fields there are a work in progress and she looks forward to spending her life cultivating them. The old farmhouse particularly tickles her. It has a wide front porch facing a sleepy corner of Chilmark and feels, she says, like the Southern porches she sat on growing up.

Last year was a good year here, and at the end of the season I decided it would be nice to gather before friends migrated in various directions for the winter. It seemed obvious that Krishana, who was happily heading nowhere, was key to my November party. Without hesitating she offered me her flower studio, an open-air stone outbuilding on her property, for our early Thanksgiving celebration. I provided fire and food; she dressed the table and walls. We ate sheltered but outside, the nip in the air making the turkey and the company all the more enjoyable.

Turkey — Divided and Conquered

Serves about 8

Brine the turkey a day in advance. Braise the legs, then make the oyster-and-herb stuffing for the breast, which I roast separately, adding just enough water to keep it juicy. You may lose the drama of carrying a big bird to the table, but you more than make up for it with flavor.

Kosher salt

2 tablespoons honey

1 free-range turkey, about 14 pounds

About 6 tablespoons neutral oil, such as canola

3 onions, chopped

Freshly ground black pepper

3 cups loosely packed parsley leaves

8 oysters, shucked

6 tablespoons butter, softened

1 lemon

Brine the turkey. Combine 6 tablespoons salt and the honey in a large pot. Add 6 cups water and bring to a boil over high heat. Give the brine a stir to make sure all the salt has dissolved, then pour it into a bowl and allow it to cool completely.

Cut the legs with thighs from the turkey and put them in the brine. Cut the wings and the breasts from the carcass, leaving the breasts whole and boneless. (If you'd rather, you can have your butcher cut off the legs and debone the breast; just make sure to ask for the bones.) Add the wings and breasts to the brine. Cover the pot and refrigerate overnight.

Make the stock. Heat the oven to 400°F. Chop the carcass in quarters. Heat a skim of oil over high heat in a flameproof roasting pan large enough to hold the carcass pieces in a single layer. Add the carcass to the pan and give the pan a shake. Transfer the pan to the oven and roast the bones, turning them once or twice, until they are evenly browned, about 1 hour. Pour off any accumulated fat. Deglaze the pan over a high flame by adding several inches of water, about 6 cups, and scraping up the "fond" (the browned bits on the bottom of the pan). Adjust the heat and simmer the stock, adding more water if it reduces by much more than a quarter. Simmer until it is flavorful, about 30 minutes. Allow the stock to cool. Strain it, and discard the bones. You should have about 4½ cups. (If you have less, that's OK; just add water or supplement with chicken stock.) The stock can be made in advance and refrigerated.

Braise the turkey legs and wings. Heat the oven to 400°F. Heat a skim of oil in a large flameproof roasting pan over medium-high heat. Add the onions and cook, stirring frequently, until they begin to brown, about 12 minutes. Remove the turkey legs and wings from the brine and arrange in a single layer over the onions. Season the turkey lightly with salt and more generously with pepper, then add the reserved stock and enough water so the liquid comes halfway up the turkey. Braise in the oven, uncovered, until the legs and thighs begin to brown, about 1 hour.

Turn the legs and wings over and cook another hour, then flip them again — adding more water to the pan as the liquid reduces. Continue braising until the legs and wings are fully tender, about 30 minutes longer. Allow the turkey to rest in the braising liquid until the stock is cool. Strain the braising liquid, then spoon the fat from the top. Reserve 4 cups of this broth for gravy (page 79) and return the rest to the pan with the braised legs and wings. Top the pan loosely with foil and reserve. The legs and wings can be braised early in the day or even a day ahead.

Roast the breast. About 2 hours before you plan to eat, heat the oven to 400°F. Remove the breast from the brine and pat dry. Prepare the oyster stuffing by first blanching the parsley leaves in boiling salted water, until just wilted, then refreshing in ice water. Squeeze excess water out, then chop the parsley finely. Chop the oysters, reserving their liquor. Combine the parsley and oysters in a bowl and mix in the butter and oyster liquor using a wooden spoon. Grate the lemon zest into the oyster mixture (use a Microplane if you have one) and then add the lemon's juice. Using your fingers, gently push about half of the butter mixture under the skin of the turkey breast. Turn the breast over and put the remaining butter between the two halves and under the tenderloins. Truss each breast with kitchen twine at regular intervals.

Lightly salt the skin of the breast. Heat a skim of oil in a small flameproof roasting pan or ovenproof skillet over high heat. Put the turkey breast in the pan, skin-side up. Add a cup of water and place the pan in the oven to roast. Cook for about 1 hour, adding water from time to time and basting every 15 minutes with pan juices, until the turkey breast is done. Test by inserting a metal skewer into the very center of the breast — if the tip is hot when removed, the turkey is done; or use an instant-read thermometer to check for an internal reading of 155°F. Pull the breast from the oven and allow it to rest for 15 minutes before slicing.

Reheat the legs and wings. When the breast comes out of the oven, remove the foil from the pan holding the legs and wings and return to the 400°F oven to heat through for 15 minutes, turning them once or twice.

Slice the breast, legs, and thighs. Arrange all the meat on a platter and serve.

Gravy

Makes about 2 cups

This gravy is thickened with sweet, caramelized onions rather than butter and flour. It is obviously a healthier way to go, but it is truly just as rich tasting and, if you like, you can make it a day ahead.

4 cups turkey broth (page 74) or chicken stock (see page 140)

About 2 tablespoons neutral oil, such as canola

3 large yellow onions, sliced

Kosher salt and freshly ground black pepper

Bring the broth or stock to a boil in a small saucepan over high heat. Allow it to simmer vigorously until reduced by about half. Meanwhile, heat the oil in a skillet over medium-low heat. Add the onions, season with salt and pepper, and cook, stirring occasionally, until they are soft and caramelized, about 40 minutes.

In a blender or food processor, puree the onions with the reduced stock. If the gravy is too thick, thin it with a little water, then season it to taste with salt and pepper. Heat over low heat immediately before serving.

Celery Root "Stuffing"

Serves 8

This is a vegetarian "stuffing" flavored with celery root, stalks, and leaves. It is the ideal accompaniment to an oyster-and-herb-stuffed turkey breast or a simple roast chicken.

2 baguettes, cubed

About 2 pounds celery root, scrubbed

12 stalks celery

2 tablespoons neutral oil, such as canola

8 tablespoons butter

2 large onions, chopped

Kosher salt

4 tablespoons chopped fresh sage

1 teaspoon lemon zest

Heat the oven to 325°F. Place the bread on a baking sheet and dry it thoroughly in the oven, about 35 minutes. Pull the bread from the oven and allow it to cool. Keep the oven on.

Peel the celery root and put the peelings in a large pot. Cut the root into large dice and reserve. Trim the celery stalks, reserving the leaves and trimmings. Add the trimmings to the pot with the root peels. Dice the celery; reserve the diced celery and leaves separately.

Add 10 cups of water to the pot with the trimmings and bring it to a boil over high heat. Reduce the heat to low and simmer the celery stock for 20 minutes.

Heat a large skillet over medium-high heat. Working in two batches, add 1 tablespoon of the oil and 2 tablespoons of the butter to the pan. When the butter melts, add half the diced celery root and cook, stirring frequently, until it begins to color slightly, about 10 minutes. Add half the onions and season with salt. Cook, continuing to stir or toss frequently, until softened, about 10 minutes. Add half the diced celery and 1 tablespoon of the chopped sage and cook until the celery is tender, about 4 minutes. Remove the skillet from the heat and add half the bread; mix well. Transfer the stuffing to a large bowl. Wipe out the skillet and repeat to cook the remaining celery root, onions, and celery, and 1 tablespoon of the sage.

Strain the celery stock. Add enough stock to the stuffing to moisten it. Start with 4 cups, adding more if the bread seems too dry—it should be spongy, not soggy. Taste the stuffing and add salt as needed. Spoon the mixture into a large buttered baking dish. Dot the top with the remaining 4 tablespoons of butter. Bake at 325°F until the stuffing is brown and the top is crisp, about 40 minutes.

Mince the remaining 2 tablespoons of sage with the reserved celery leaves and the lemon zest. Sprinkle the sage mixture over the stuffing and serve warm.

Pot-Roasted Pheasant with Bread

Serves 8

The pheasants here are pot-roasted over onions and bread. You wind up creating a tasty simple "stuffing" in the pot as you cook the birds.

Kosher salt

1 tablespoon honey

2 pheasants, 2 to 2½ pounds each

About 6 tablespoons butter, softened

Freshly ground black pepper

4 sprigs rosemary

About 2 tablespoons neutral oil, such as canola

2 onions, quartered

1 baguette, cut into 8 pieces (spit the baguette lengthwise, then cut each half into 4 pieces)

A day ahead, combine 3 tablespoons salt with the honey and 2 gallons water in a large pot and bring to a boil over high heat. When the water boils, stir to make sure the salt dissolves, then set the brine aside to cool completely. Put the pheasants, breast-side down, in a large bowl (or pot). Pour the brine over the birds, cover, and refrigerate overnight.

About 2 hours before you plan to eat, heat the oven to 425°F. Remove the pheasants from the brine and let them air dry for 15 minutes. Rub them with about 4 tablespoons of the softened butter then season lightly with salt (they've already been brined) and more generously with pepper. Put 2 sprigs rosemary in the cavity of each bird.

Heat a skim of oil over high heat in a deep skillet or Dutch oven large enough to contain the birds (if you don't have a pan that big, cook each pheasant in its own). Add the onions to the pan, then the bread, cut-side down. Let the bread toast a minute or so, then add the pheasants, breast-side up.

Transfer the pan to the oven and roast the birds until they begin to color, about 25 minutes. Pull the pan out of the oven and add a cup or so of

water—enough to moisten the drippings in the pan and create a "jus." Baste the birds with the jus and return the pan to the oven. Continue roasting until the pheasants are cooked—the joints are no longer tight and the juices run clear, about 15 minutes more. Take the pan from the oven, cover it, and allow the pheasants to steam for 40 minutes.

Just before you are ready to serve, transfer the pheasants to a cutting board. Take the bread from the pan, cut into manageable pieces, and put in a bowl. Add the roasted onion from the pan and toss with the bread. Season the "stuffing" with salt and pepper to taste. Reserve the pan with the drippings and browned bits.

Carve the pheasants, cutting off the legs and wings first and then the breasts. Slice each breast into three pieces. Arrange the "stuffing" on a platter. Put the pheasant on top and season with salt and pepper.

Chop the carcass and add it to the pan. Turn the flame to high and deglaze with about ½ cup of water—just enough to loosen the "fond," the browned bits, from the pan. Let the water boil for a minute. When the pan sauce is concentrated, reduce the heat and stir in a tablespoon (or two) of butter. Season, then strain the "jus" over the pheasant and serve.

Mashed Potatoes

The secret to perfect mashed potatoes is not overworking them (and using plenty of butter).

8 medium Yukon gold potatoes, peeled

Kosher salt

¾ cup milk

1 pound (4 sticks) butter

Put the potatoes in a large pot. Add water to cover, season with salt, and bring to a boil over high heat. Reduce the heat and simmer until the potatoes are easily pierced with a fork, about 15 minutes. Drain the potatoes.

Warm the milk with the butter in a small pot over low heat. Use a ricer to puree the potatoes (if you don't have a ricer, quickly grate the potatoes by hand) one at a time into a large bowl, adding and incorporating the milk mixture as you go until they are as creamy as you like. Adjust the seasoning with salt and serve.

Salt-Baked Sweet Potatoes

Serves 8

In November the island's sweet potatoes are coming into their own after weeks of ripening in root cellars. They are so sweet that when you bake them, caramel lines their skins. I roast mine in salt to concentrate the sweet flavor.

> 8 medium sweet potatoes
> About 8 cups kosher salt
> 6 sprigs rosemary, broken

Heat the oven to 400°F. Scrub the potatoes. Mix the salt with enough water so that it clumps and holds together, about 1 cup. Spread half the salt mixture in a baking dish large enough to hold the potatoes in a single, nicely spaced layer. Put 2 of the rosemary sprigs on the salt. Put the potatoes on top. Lay the rest of the rosemary over the potatoes, then cover with salt, packing it around the sides. The potatoes don't need to be sealed in salt, but you want them blanketed (mix more salt with a little water if it is necessary to get the job done). Bake the potatoes until they are tender when squeezed, about 1 hour and 20 minutes.

Remove the potatoes from the oven. Brush off the salt and rosemary and serve. You can bake the sweet potatoes a day in advance and reheat in a 350°F oven for about 30 minutes.

Cranberry Sauce

Makes about 3 cups

Combining dried cherries with fresh cranberries brings out the best in both.

8 ounces dried cherries

1 cup Prosecco or other sparkling wine

1 pound fresh cranberries, rinsed and picked through

About 2 teaspoons sugar

Kosher salt and freshly ground black pepper

Bring the cherries and Prosecco to a boil in a small saucepan over high heat. Remove the pan from the heat and let the cherries steep in the wine until they are plump, about 15 minutes.

Combine the cranberries and sugar in a food processor. Pulse the machine until the cranberries are coarsely chopped (or you can hand chop them). Transfer the chopped cranberries to a bowl. Add the dried cherry mixture and mix well. Season to taste with salt and pepper and serve.

Pickled Peppers and Green Tomatoes

I use the same recipe to pickle various peppers and green tomatoes. You can pickle each vegetable separately, or do as I do and combine the tomatoes and a spicy pepper like a cherry bomb. I find this adds spice to the tomatoes and flavor to the peppers.

> About 8 peppers, depending on size; try Anaheim, poblanos, cherry bombs, or jalapeños
>
> 3 to 6 small green tomatoes
>
> 1½ cups Champagne vinegar
>
> 3 tablespoons sugar
>
> 1 star anise
>
> 1½ tablespoons kosher salt

Discard the stems and seeds of the peppers and cut away the ribs. Cut larger peppers like Anaheims and poblanos in half, then into lengths. Smaller peppers like cherry bombs, sweet cherry peppers, and small jalapeños can be left whole. Core the tomatoes and cut them in sixths or eighths, depending on their size.

Combine the vinegar, sugar, star anise, salt, and 1½ cups water in a large pot. Bring it to a boil over high heat. Stir to make sure the salt and sugar dissolve, then remove the pot from the stove. Add the peppers immediately. Wait to add the tomatoes (if using) until the liquid has cooled to warm. Set aside for at least 2 hours. Remove the peppers and tomatoes from the pickling liquid and serve, or cover and refrigerate.

Caramelized Brussels Sprouts

Serves 8

One of my favorite smells in the world is the aroma of caramelizing Brussels sprouts, followed closely by the sweet odor of charring cauliflower. Cabbage and broccoli both also smell delicious to me, though maybe not quite as earthy. These vegetables, all stalwarts at my Thanksgiving table, are members of the *Brassica* family (also known as *Cruciferae*). Browning *Brassica* sugars is what produces that smell I love. The secret, I've found, is cutting the vegetable to expose the protected interiors and create flat surfaces to maintain even contact with the pan. For a big crowd you will probably need to use two pans or work in batches. I like to get all my sprouts seared off an hour or so before I plan to serve, then give them a warm up in a hot skillet or the oven just before I put them on the table.

> 1 to 2 tablespoons neutral oil, such as canola
> About 2 pounds Brussels sprouts, trimmed and halved through the core
> Kosher salt
> 4 sprigs thyme (optional)
> About 2 tablespoons freshly squeezed lemon juice

Rub a large cold skillet (or two) with the oil. Arrange the Brussels sprouts cut-side down in the oiled pan. Turn the heat to high, season with plenty of salt, and cook the sprouts until you can smell the sugars caramelizing, about 5 minutes. Reduce the heat to low and continue cooking until the cut side of each is nicely browned, about 12 minutes. Add thyme, if using, then flip the Brussels sprouts and continue cooking until they are just cooked through, about 5 minutes more. Season with lemon juice and additional salt and serve.

Caramelized Apple Tart

Makes 1 (12-inch) tart

I like to serve this tart—a version of the classic *tarte Tatin,* warm. If you make it ahead of time, leave it in the pan, then reheat it for 20 minutes or so in a 375°F oven before turning it out onto a platter to serve.

4 tablespoons butter

½ cup sugar

Pinch of salt

3 medium eating apples, peeled, cored, and thinly sliced

Flaky Pastry Dough (page 92); or 1 (14-ounce) package frozen puff pastry, defrosted

Heat the oven to 400°F. Combine the butter, sugar, and salt in a 12-inch cast-iron skillet. Heat over medium, stirring occasionally. As the sugar melts and begins to brown, stir more frequently. Lower the heat a little if necessary to keep the caramel from bubbling over. Cook the caramel until it is deep amber, then remove it from the heat and let it cool in the skillet. Arrange the apples in an overlapping single layer on the caramel.

Roll out the pastry dough on a lightly floured board to a round just a little bigger than the pan and about ⅛ inch thick. Lay the pastry over the apples, tucking it around them into the skillet. Cut several vents in the pastry to allow steam to escape. Bake the tart until the pastry is a deep golden brown, about 35 minutes.

Take the pan out of the oven and allow it to cool until the caramel is no longer molten, about 5 minutes. Loosen the edges with a spatula then carefully invert the tart onto a plate and serve.

Flaky Pastry Dough

Makes enough dough for 1 (12-inch) tart

I find this recipe more forgiving than traditional puff pastry, but, like the original, it does take some time—preparing it is a four-step process. Save any leftover scraps and bake them dusted with sugar and serve alone or with ice cream.

½ pound (2 sticks) cold butter

2 cups all-purpose flour

1 teaspoon salt

¼ to ½ cup ice water

Dice the butter and combine it with the flour and salt in a bowl. Toss the ingredients together and refrigerate for 15 minutes.

Using a pastry cutter or your fingers, gradually work in enough water so the dough can just be gathered together—like a rough pie dough. Using your hands, shape the dough into a rectangle, then wrap it in plastic wrap and refrigerate for at least 1 hour.

Roll the dough out on a floured work surface into a rectangle about ¼ inch thick. (Don't worry if it is crumbly, simply fill in gaps with scraps, it doesn't have to be perfect.) Fold the dough in thirds (like a letter). Rotate the dough a quarter turn so the folds are vertical rather than horizontal. Roll out the dough again, then again fold it in thirds. Return it to the fridge for another hour. Repeat this procedure of rolling, folding, and refrigerating 2 more times. Wrap and refrigerate overnight or freeze.

Late Harvest 93

Squash Tart

Makes 1 (10-inch) tart

Almost any winter squash will work here — hubbard, kabocha, butternut, or, of course, a sweet orange sugar pumpkin.

FOR THE DOUGH

½ cup (1 stick) butter

¾ cup all-purpose flour

¼ cup whole wheat flour

¼ cup cornmeal

2 teaspoons sugar

Pinch of salt

About ¼ cup ice water

FOR THE FILLING

1 small to medium winter squash, about 1 pound (you want 2 cups cooked squash)

2 eggs

¼ cup sugar

4 tablespoons butter, melted then cooled

½ cup maple syrup

1 cup crème fraîche (see Maple Crème Fraîche Ice Cream, page 160, for how to make your own)

¼ teaspoon powdered ginger

⅛ teaspoon ground cardamom

Prepare the dough. Combine the butter, all-purpose flour, whole wheat flour, cornmeal, sugar, salt, and water in a food processor. Pulse just until the dough forms coarse crumbs. (To mix by hand, mix the flours, cornmeal, sugar, salt, and water together, then cut in the butter using a pastry cutter or two knives.) Gather the dough into a ball, wrap in plastic, and chill for at least 1 hour.

Roast the squash for the filling. Heat the oven to 375°F. Split the squash, remove the seeds (these are good toasted, see page 145), and place the squash cut-side down in a baking dish. Add about ¼ inch of water and roast until tender, about 45 minutes. Let the squash cool for a few minutes. Scoop the flesh out of the shell and measure out 2 cups for the filling. (Reserve any leftover for another purpose.)

On a lightly floured surface, roll out the chilled dough to a 14-inch round about ⅛ inch thick. Fit into a 10-inch tart pan. Cover the dough with plastic and chill once more.

Finish the filling. Whisk the eggs with the sugar, then whisk in the melted butter. Whisk in the syrup, crème fraîche, ginger, and cardamom. Mash the squash then stir it into the egg mixture. Beat to combine.

Pour the filling into the chilled shell. Bake the tart at 375°F until the filling is puffed and gently set and the crust is golden, about 40 minutes. Allow the tart to cool, then slice and serve.

A Christmas Brunch

blueberry pancakes and sausage

salted fish and scrambled eggs

kale and pork belly

concord grape bellini

SALTING FISH

About Cod Fish :: *How they are* **Caught, Cured, and Packed.**

VINEYARD HAVEN, MARTHA'S VINEYARD, MASS.

Dear Sir:—I will try to explain how my Fish are caught, cured, and packed.

The fish are caught at a small island called Noman's Land, which is situated seven miles south of Gay Head. The fishermen fish from small boats, which are sharp on each end, like the one represented in the cut. The boats are called Noman's Land boats, because they are built for use there. The sharp stern is so they can be launched stern first in rough weather. They range in length from fourteen to twenty-one feet, and are hauled up the beach, on skids, by a yoke of oxen every night. The fish are caught on rocky ledges surrounding the island, brought ashore and cleaned and washed, then taken into the fish stores, split, and put to soak in tubs of clean water in order to take out all the blood. The next morning they are scrubbed to take off what blood may adhere to them, rinsed off and salted with the best salt to be had. When salted enough the fish are washed again, the black nape-skins removed, then spread to dry on a point of stones called "Stony Point," which is composed entirely of small stones which have been washed up by the sea. When dry they are tied up in bundles of fifty (50) pounds each, and so taken to market.

These fish when dry are as white as snow, and as clean as it is possible to make them. I claim they are cleaner and better than any bank fish, which are caught and salted down in the hold, there to remain until the vessel reaches the home port.

I take these fish, skin them, remove all the bones, and pack them in three-pound boxes, or "other sizes if desired," lined with waxed paper. I take the greatest care to pack nothing but perfect fish, throwing out everything that does not come up to the desired quality.

They have fished from Noman's Land for more than a hundred years.

Yours truly,

ALBERT O. FISCHER.

Poppy's father, named, like him, Albert Oswald Fischer, was born in 1875 in Montclair, New Jersey. He went to school on Nantucket, then married Ethel Luce. She was born on Martha's Vineyard and traced her lineage back to Henry Luce, who settled here in 1670. Albert liked farming but was good at many other things, and

Ethel came from strong island stock and knew how to make do—which was lucky because Albert and Ethel lived during the lean years that began after the collapse of the whaling industry and continued through the first half of the twentieth century, as the island's economy was pinched and pained by the wars in Europe and by the Great Depression. In spite of it all, Albert and his brother established and ran the successful fish salting business he describes in his letter above.

He concentrated his efforts on cod, then plentiful. Salt cod fetched a high price in the domestic market and an even higher price overseas. If his claims are to be believed, his product was of the highest quality. I am struck by his conscious fishing practices, how he took the best, freshest product and treated it with the utmost respect. He advertised fishing in small boats every day and he relied on the bright sun and the clean wind to cure his fish.

Atlantic cod have been overfished. Although it is still possible to catch them here, it is rare. I buy cod now only when I know the fisherman, and then I eat it fresh. I've never salted cod, but I do salt other fish. It is easy and the ideal solution when you have caught more than you can eat or see a bargain at the market.

I don't really have a recipe, but you don't really need one. Start with the freshest possible fish fillets. I prefer to salt white-fleshed fish like fluke, flounder, sole, striped bass, or black sea bass. Soak the fillets overnight in clean, cold water. If your water is treated with chlorine or fluoride or is questionable in any way, use bottled spring water.

The next day, rinse the fillets in more fresh water and then pack them in salt. Put a generous layer on the bottom of a large, flat-bottomed container. Arrange a single layer of fish on the salt, then cover the fillets with another layer of salt. Make sure the fillets are entirely surrounded by the salt. You can do several layers if you need to. Cover the container tightly and refrigerate. The salt will draw the moisture from the fish. Cure the fish until it is firm (not hard) and no longer seems "raw." With a thin fillet, like fluke or sole, 24 hours is sufficient. A thicker, denser fillet like striped bass will take longer, at least 48 hours. With larger fillets, change the salt when it becomes saturated—every 24 hours or so.

Unpack the fillets and rinse them in clean water. Then dry them. With small fillets you can punch a hole in the top, thread a piece of twine through the hole, and hang the fillet in the refrigerator for 24 hours (in the winter you can hang fillets in a screened porch). With larger fillets it is easier to lay them on a rack set over a baking pan to air-dry, uncovered in the refrigerator (air circulation is key), turning them over from time to time.

Once the fish is dried, pack the fillets into an airtight container and store them in the refrigerator until you need them. To use, rehydrate the fillets by soaking them for 12 to 24 hours — taste a piece to see that the fish tastes slightly salted but not too salty. At this point the fish can be used in place of soaked salt cod. I like salted fish many ways, but it is delicious simply fried — a great meal anytime and particularly nice for breakfast during the holidays.

Pan-Fried Salted Fish

Serves 4

By varying the oil (or fat) you use to fry, you can get quite different effects. Fried in light, clean-tasting oil the fish will be delicate, perfect with a salad. But substitute sausage or bacon drippings and you will have fried fish you simply can't stop eating—ideal for brunch. Salt cod is also good prepared this way.

> 2 fillets salted bass, about 4 ounces each
>
> About 2 tablespoons neutral oil, such as canola (or sausage drippings)

Soak the fish in several changes of water for 12 to 24 hours—the best way to gauge whether the fish is ready to cook is to cut off a sliver and taste it. If it tastes lightly salted, it is ready, otherwise continue soaking.

Dry the fish with paper towels. Heat a medium skillet over high heat. Add enough oil to coat the pan, then add the fish, skin-side down. Cook, pressing the fillets flat with the back of a spatula, until the skin is golden, about 2 minutes. Flip the fillets and cook until the second sides are also nicely colored, about 2 minutes more, then serve.

EGGS 101 — SCRAMBLING AND FRYING

Some aficionados scramble eggs gently in a double boiler; I don't have the patience and don't think it's necessary. I scramble my eggs in a frying pan in butter and the whole production takes less time than it takes to beat the eggs. I am quick but careful.

Heat a small heavy-bottomed skillet over medium heat. You want the surface of the pan uniformly hot, so take the time to let the heat radiate and distribute. For one person, crack 2 eggs into a bowl and whip them for 1 minute — time it and you'll find this is surprisingly long, but it makes all the difference. Really beating the eggs in the first place allows you to work fast over the stove and still wind up with creamy eggs.

When your eggs are beaten, add a knob of butter to the skillet. Wait until the butter is foaming, then add a healthy pinch of salt and a few cracks of pepper to the eggs and pour them into the pan. Let them set up a bit as they bubble and begin to firm up in a single layer on the bottom of the pan; then, using a rubber spatula, working in a circular motion, start stirring the eggs, covering the entire area of the pan, spiraling in and out. Fold the ribbons of barely cooked egg over and into themselves. Move more quickly as the eggs begin coming together, lifting the pan a couple of inches off the flame as you work if the skillet seems like it's getting too hot. Continue stirring, plowing the just barely cooked, firm, pale yellow egg into the still runny egg. As you cook, the scramble will go quickly from the consistency of loose porridge to custard. At this point remove the pan from the heat. Turn the eggs over once or twice more, then scoop them onto a warm plate and eat them immediately, seasoned with freshly cracked pepper and a little chopped fresh chervil if you have some.

To fry eggs, I also preheat the skillet, but over a higher heat. Starting with a hot skillet prevents the eggs from sticking and helps keep them tender. I add a slosh of oil — a neutral oil like canola or a light olive oil. I don't use butter because it burns in a hot pan. Swirl the oil around until the surface of the skillet is evenly coated. Then pour off the excess, leaving an even film.

I crack eggs, one at a time, into the hot oil, then reduce the heat to medium. I season the eggs with salt, some cracked pepper, and crushed red pepper if I'm in the mood. Then I let the eggs fry undisturbed until they are set on the bottom, about 3 minutes total, playing with the heat: 1 minute over medium heat, then 1 minute over medium-low, then another minute over low. When the whites are just about set all the way through, I turn off the stove, cover the pan with a tight-fitting lid, and let the eggs "rest" for 1 minute, until the whites are cooked completely but the yolks are runny.

Breakfast Sausage Patties

Serves 4

The past few years a friend of mine has been tapping maples around the woods of Chilmark. I've been enjoying his syrup, which is light in color and almost floral tasting. I use a little in my sausage mix, which makes them go nicely with pancakes. As with any homemade sausage, it's a good idea to fry off a bit to test that the seasoning is where you want it.

> ½ pound ground pork
>
> 2 ounces lardo (or other fresh or cured pork fat), chilled and diced
>
> 2 tablespoons finely chopped fresh sage
>
> 2 teaspoons maple syrup
>
> Kosher salt and freshly ground black pepper
>
> About 1 tablespoon neutral oil, such as canola

Combine the pork, lardo, sage, and maple syrup in a mixing bowl. Season the mixture with plenty of salt and pepper and mix well. Form the sausage mixture into 4 patties.

Heat a skim of oil in a large skillet over medium-high heat. Add the sausage patties and fry, cooking and browning on both sides until they are no longer pink inside, about 8 minutes, then serve.

Blueberry Pancakes

Serves 4

Tiny wild blueberries grow on bushes all over the north shore of the island. As kids, we'd pick with pails tied around our necks. We'd eat our fill then freeze the rest for the pies and pancakes we enjoyed all winter long. I find that the trick to good pancakes is taking the time to get your pan evenly heated. I use a cast-iron skillet and put it on to warm up while I make the batter.

1½ cups all-purpose flour

½ cup whole wheat flour

1 tablespoon baking powder

1 tablespoon sugar

Pinch salt

2 eggs

4 tablespoons butter, melted and cooled; plus about 2 tablespoons butter for the pan

About 2 cups buttermilk

1½ cups fresh blueberries, picked through

Maple syrup

Heat a large cast-iron skillet over medium heat.

Prepare the batter. Mix the all-purpose flour, whole wheat flour, baking powder, sugar, and salt in a large bowl. In a separate bowl, beat the eggs with the melted butter, then stir in the buttermilk. Add the wet ingredients to the dry ingredients, stirring just enough to mix the two but no more than that—a few lumps are much better than over-beaten batter. Gently fold in the blueberries.

Melt about a tablespoon of butter in the heated skillet. Drop batter, a generous spoonful at a time, into the pan. Cook the pancakes until they bubble and begin to firm up at their edges, about 3 minutes, then flip and cook until the second side is golden, about 2 minutes more. Repeat until the batter runs out. Serve the pancakes warm with maple syrup.

Pan-Roasted Pork Belly with Kale

Serves 4

Sometimes I prefer the direct meatiness of uncured belly for breakfast instead of traditional bacon. Caramelized and browned but not necessarily crisped, it makes for a nice, hearty counterpoint to blanched greens, which I really love in the morning.

About 1 tablespoon neutral oil, such as canola

½ pound pork belly, cut in half lengthwise and then into ¼-inch slices (do it yourself or ask your butcher)

Kosher salt

1 pound Tuscan kale, stems trimmed

Half a lemon

Heat the barest skim of oil in a skillet large enough to hold the pork belly in a single layer over medium heat. When the oil is warm enough to coat the pan, add the slices of pork. Reduce the heat to low and begin rendering the fat. Cook until the first sides are beginning to color, about 15 minutes, then flip the belly slices and cook until the second sides are golden brown, about 15 minutes more. Pour off excess fat as you cook; reserve it for another purpose (I like to use it to fry potatoes). Flip the slices a final time and finish browning the meat over low heat, a final 15 minutes or so. Pull the pan off the heat and let the pork rest in the warm rendered fat.

Bring a pot of salted water to a boil. Add the kale and blanch until tender, 3 to 5 minutes. Drain the kale, transfer to a bowl, and arrange the pork on top. Squeeze the lemon half into the pan you cooked the pork in, swirl it around, then pour it over the belly and kale and serve.

Concord Grape Bellinis

Makes 4 to 6

Concord grape syrup is a good starting point for cocktails. I also like to use it in cooking both sweet and savory dishes. So when the grapes are ripe I make big batches using this simple ratio: 1 pound of grapes to 1 cup of water, plus sugar to taste. You can use the same ratio and method to make beach plum syrup.

FOR THE CONCORD GRAPE SYRUP
About 3 tablespoons sugar
1 pound Concord grapes, rinsed well

FOR THE COCKTAILS
1 bottle Prosecco or other sparkling wine

Make the syrup. Combine the sugar and 1 cup water in a large pot and bring to a boil over high heat. Add the grapes, stirring and pressing them down lightly with a wooden spoon. Reduce the heat slightly, cover the pot, and simmer until the grapes begin to soften and burst, about 10 minutes. Take the pot off the heat and allow the contents to cool thoroughly.

Mash the grapes with a wooden spoon, then strain through a double layer of cheesecloth into a small pot, squeezing out every last bit of juice. Bring the syrup to a boil, then allow it to reduce until it concentrates and you are left with about 1 cup of grape syrup. Taste the syrup and adjust the sweetness with sugar while it is warm. Allow the syrup to cool, then chill it.

Make the cocktails. Put a tablespoon of chilled syrup into each of 4 to 6 Champagne glasses. Fill the glasses with Prosecco and serve. (Freeze the remaining syrup or have another round.)

TWELVE GENERATIONS ON MARTHA'S VINEYARD

Henry Luce, 1640–1687/1689, married Remember Litchfield

Robert b. 1667; Remember b. 1670; Israel b. 1671; Experience b. 1673; Eleazer b. 1675; Henry b. 1677;
Thomas b. 1679; William b. 1681; David b. 1683; Josiah b. 1685

Robert Luce, 1667–1711/1714, married Desire Norton

Judith b. 1689; Henry b. 1690; Samuel b. 1692; Jonathan b. 1696; Desire b. 1700; Mary b. 1701; Mercy b. 1703

Henry Luce, 1690–1769, married Hannah Merry

Eleazaer b. 1711; Joanna b. 1714; Robert b. 1715; Adonijah b. 1717; Jonathan b. 1722; Abraham b. 1723;
Isaac b. 1726; Peter b. 1730; Jacob b. 1734

Jonathan Luce, 1722–1791, married Urania ?

Joana b. 1744; Ruth b. 1745; Samuel b. 1752; Malachi b. 1755; Shubael b. 1757; Urana b. 1760; Solomon b. 1762;
Damaris b. 1764; Nancy b. 1766; Ruhama b.1768

Malachi Luce, 1755–1838, married Anna Cathcart Luce, married Anna Weeks

Priscilla b. 1780/2; Shubael b. 1783; Arvin b. 1787; Love b. 1790; Cathcart b. 1792; Rumah b. 1798

Shubael Luce, 1783–1853, married Betsy Smith

Cordelia b. 1812; Emeline b. 1816; Anna b. 1818; John Adams b. 1824

Capt. John A. Luce, 1824–1903, married Mary Norton Lambert

Elisha Lambert b. 1849; John Osborn b. 1855; Annie Arnold b. 1868

Elisha Lambert Luce, 1849–1922, married Lois Starbuck Look

Viola May b. 1881; Ethel Morton b. 1883; Aurilla Jeanette b. 1893

Ethel Morton Luce, 1883–1976, married Albert O. Fischer, Sr., 1875–1961

Frederick O. b. 1913; Albert Oswald b. 1914; Arnold M. b. 1915; Lois b. 1917

Albert O. Fischer, Jr., 1914–2011, married Regina McLaughlin b.1915

Douglas b. 1941; Marie b. 1942; Suzanne b. 1945; Albert Oswald b. 1949

Albert O. Fischer, III, b.1949, married Jean Wallace, 1951-2005, married Linda Baci

Andrew b. 1978; Christopher b. 1980; Lydia b. 1990; Molly b. 1992

DEEP FREEZE

scallop crudo
fennel, feta, mint
rigatoni, clams
chocolate tart

birthday dinner
january third

SCALLOPS

We met well before first light — he wanted to get out on Menemsha Pond early. The pond flows across the border between the towns of Chilmark and Aquinnah, and my captain, a bold and impetuous member of the Larsen family, was licensed only in Chilmark. The year he took me out hadn't been a great one for scallops, so his plan was to take a few pre-dawn tows on the Aquinnah side where there was less competition and it was rumored the bottom was covered with easy pickings.

We set out from his mooring, our lights extinguished, the only sign of our mission the purr of his outboard. We headed into Aquinnah and dropped the net. We made three passes, quickly filling our dredges. Then we saw the flash of headlights once, then again. We were caught.

Bay scallops thrive in our clean, cold waters and they always fetch top dollar (off-island they're often tagged as "Nantucket bay scallops" to warrant premium prices). The price of bays fluctuates from just shy of twenty dollars per pound to highs of over thirty-five. But sold high or sold low, scallops are always valuable and fishing rights are taken very seriously.

I quickly understood that the flashed warning was not to be trifled with. My usually fearless leader wheeled the boat around and motored quickly back across the line to Chilmark. We worked on, now careful to remain within the confines of the fisheries law, reaching the two-bushel limit quickly enough to wave at the second boat out that morning on our way in. We were eager to sell our haul and expected a good price, just as my grandmother Rena had when she took to the winter waters of the pond.

Rena was an off-islander, working in Edgartown for the summer when she met my grandfather, Ozzie. They met at a dance in Chilmark in 1938. She'd gone with a date. Ozzie wasn't alone either, so he waited until she was alone, then walked up and asked her for a dance. Ozzie had hitched his pants up with a length of rope, and so Rena declined. Undaunted, my grandfather retorted, "Columbus took a chance. Why don't you?" In the end she did.

They got married, reared their kids, did their jobs, and lived what my father calls "the easy life" up-island, putting their extra time and energy into taking care of their own plot. It was a good and happy existence. But there was a growing bone of contention as the years went on. Rena was unhappy that they didn't have a TV.

She wound up many evenings watching boxing with her friend Mrs. Morgan. Mrs. Morgan, a spirited Scotswoman, liked the fights and would jump up swinging at the set, exclaiming, "Kick his arse!" as if the boxers on the little screen might respond. Rena enjoyed the evenings with her feisty friend, but wanted a set of her own. She and Ozzie discussed it; money was too tight. Then Rena came up with a plan, and scallops were the key.

Rena explained her scheme to her husband and, much as he might have liked to, Ozzie (a very reluctant seaman) couldn't think of a reason to object. So she marched herself over to the town hall and bought a pair of scallop permits. She told her friend Eileen Mayhew what they were up to. Eileen thought the idea sounded fine and she and her husband joined. They spent the rest of the winter dragging for scallops as a foursome. Rena says it was really cold, colder than it is now, and she'd come home frozen and aching from head to toe from culling and shucking, but it was worth it. She sold enough scallops her first season to watch TV in her own living room by springtime.

Scallop Crudo with Fennel Fronds and Toasted Almonds

Serves 4

Bay scallops are expensive because they are extremely perishable. But when fresh, they are sweet in a way that only seafood from clean, cold water can be. I like to eat them as you would an oyster, just pried from the shell, wriggling a bit in the palm of your hand, then popped as-is into your mouth. If you find scallops in the shell or just shucked, eat them raw with or without a little embellishment.

½ teaspoon minced jalapeño

½ teaspoon minced lemon zest

½ teaspoon chopped toasted almonds

Sea salt

3 tablespoons extra-virgin olive oil

16 fresh bay scallops, shucked

2 cups loosely packed fennel fronds

About 3 tablespoons neutral oil, such as canola

Combine the minced jalapeño and lemon zest in a small bowl. Add the chopped almonds and season lightly with salt. Add the olive oil, mix, and set aside.

Using the back of a knife, "smash" each scallop just enough so it spreads open. Arrange the scallops on serving plates and season lightly with salt.

Cut the fennel fronds into delicate, feathery pieces, trimming away any thick or tough bits. Heat the neutral oil in a small skillet over medium-high heat. When the oil is hot (check it with a drop of water; if it sizzles immediately the oil is ready to go) add the fronds and fry until crisp, about 4 seconds. Using a slotted spoon, transfer them to a plate lined with a paper towel. Dress the scallops with the jalapeño mixture; finish with the frizzled fronds, and serve.

CRACK RICE

If I am not going to eat scallops raw I like to use them economically. I chop them for this dish, which we jokingly dubbed "crack rice" because we couldn't stop eating it. Heat a big skillet (or a wok if you have one) over medium-high heat. Add a trace of oil — olive or canola — then 2 ounces of slivered pancetta or bacon. When the pork begins to render its fat and become crisp, add about 2½ teaspoons minced garlic and 2 teaspoons coriander seeds (fresh if you can find them!). Keep everything in the pan moving and cook until the garlic is fragrant (a minute or so), then add a big pinch of crushed red pepper, and about 6 ounces diced bay scallops. Give everything a stir and cook just long enough to make sure all the scallop pieces are touched by the heat of the pan — they will start to whiten — then add 4 cups cooked long-grain rice. Continue cooking, keeping the contents of the pan moving as you heat (without browning) the rice. Season the rice with lemon juice and salt, finish with a handful of fresh cilantro leaves, and serve to 4 deserving friends.

Shaved Fennel, Mint, and Feta Salad

Serves 4

In the winter I crave salad, and this combination of raw fennel and mint is a favorite when it seems it will never be warm outside again. I make it different ways. I sometimes add Pickled Onions (page 282), but I always include feta. I use a local cow's milk variety. It's less tangy and salty than sheep's or goat's milk feta, but either will work; just be sure to taste as you go to get the balance right.

1 large fennel bulb

½ cup fresh mint leaves

Kosher salt

About 1 tablespoon extra-virgin olive oil

About 1 tablespoon freshly squeezed lemon juice

4 ounces feta cheese

Freshly ground black pepper

Trim off the bottom from the fennel bulb and the fronds and stalks. Peel away the outer layer if it looks old or bruised. Cut the bulb in half lengthwise (I leave the core in but you don't have to). Lay the fennel halves cut-side down on a cutting board and shave very, very thin slices, with the grain and following the round contours of the bulb lengthwise. Put the sliced fennel in a bowl. Add the mint. Season the salad with salt, mix it, then dress it with olive oil and lemon juice to taste. Toss well and arrange the salad on plates. Crumble feta over each salad, season with pepper, and serve.

CLAMMING IN THE COLD

January is the real beginning not only of the cold but of the quiet. The oaks and field grasses fade from their earlier glory to a muted beauty, turning shades of grey in reserved harmony with the old stone walls. The roads empty before the sun falls below the horizon, and headlights become lonely after the construction crews head back down-island. You leave the last street light in West Tisbury when you drive up North or South Road toward Chilmark and it is dark. On a clear night, the moonrise is something you notice, because of the shadows at Beetlebung Corner. Most prefer to admire from inside, through a window — reluctant to brace against the damp air. Night or day, in January it's tempting to stay near a fire (my smartest friends keep woodstoves in their workshops).

But crisp winter light is what I need to get through this hushed time of year. And clamming, it turns out, is the perfect January activity. On the water, I enjoy the weather rather than resist it, so my father and I meet at Menemsha Pond at low tide. The pond is busy even in winter; there are always scallopers chugging through the cold. But we are likely the only ones raking for clams along the shore, because clams aren't worth much at market.

You don't need a lot of equipment to clam. My dad provides the rakes and baskets. In the summer he likes to don a mask and dive and snack in the sun. In January, though, we stick to our work, wearing waders and gloves, to staunch the chill. We suit up, wade in, and dig for about half an hour — plenty long, hip-deep in freezing water. We take clams of all sizes — littlenecks, topnecks, quahogs, and chowders, I like them all — and don't mind waiting to figure out what to do with them until after we see what we've got.

Clam Pasta

Serves 4 to 6

My dad used to have a primitive shucking apparatus he kept on the porch—
it opened the clams but never failed to chop the bellies in half in the
process. I like to chop large hard-shell clams (quahogs) for this dish, so that
old machine would come in handy. If you'd prefer, you can steam open
smaller hard-shell clams (littlenecks) and then chop them. But either way,
don't add the clam liquor to the sauce—it will give it a metallic taste.

1 medium fennel bulb, trimmed and sliced

3 cloves garlic, 2 unpeeled and 1 peeled

Kosher salt

About 3 tablespoons extra-virgin olive oil, plus a high-quality olive
   oil to finish

4 ounces pancetta (or unsmoked bacon), cut into thin lengths

2 medium shallots, sliced

Generous pinch crushed red pepper

12 ounces rigatoni

1½ tablespoons butter

5 large quahogs, shucked and chopped; or 4 dozen littleneck clams,
   steamed open, shucked, and chopped

1 small bunch fresh flat-leaf parsley, leaves picked from half and the
   remaining chopped

About 2 teaspoons minced lemon zest

About ¾ cup homemade bread crumbs, toasted

Freshly ground black pepper

Bring a large pot of salted water to a boil over high heat. Add the fennel, the
2 unpeeled garlic cloves, and salt. Blanch until the fennel is tender, about
3 minutes. Using a slotted spoon, remove the fennel and garlic from the
water. Peel the garlic and puree it in a food processor with the fennel,
adding a little water to smooth the puree. Set aside. Reserve the boiling
water for the pasta.

Cut the remaining garlic clove in half. Sliver half and mince the rest of it; set aside separately. Heat a large skillet over high heat. Add a skim of oil, about a tablespoon, and then add the pancetta, shallots, and crushed pepper. Give the pan a swirl, then turn the heat down to medium. Cook, stirring frequently, until the pancetta is rendered and browned, about 5 minutes. Add the slivered garlic, turn the heat down, and cook, stirring it frequently, until the garlic is toasted, about 1 minute.

Add the pasta to the boiling water. Stir a couple of times to keep the rigatoni from clumping. Cook for 10 to 12 minutes, until al dente.

When the pasta is three-fourths done, about 7 minutes, finish the sauce. Add the fennel puree, the butter, and 1 tablespoon olive oil to the skillet with the pancetta. If you are using *raw* clams, add them now so they have a few minutes to cook. Season the sauce lightly with salt, then raise the heat to high and cook until the sauce is bubbling and reduces slightly, about 2 minutes. Add pasta water as necessary to keep the sauce loose; you want it moist enough to coat the pasta — a ragu.

If you are using *steamed littlenecks*, add them to the sauce when the pasta is al dente. Using a slotted spoon, lift the pasta out of the water and into the sauce. Stir or toss to combine, adding more pasta water if necessary to loosen the sauce enough to coat the rigatoni. Add the parsley leaves and toss again. Add the chopped garlic and lemon zest to the sauce. Taste for seasoning and adjust with salt.

Spoon the rigatoni onto warm plates. Top each portion with bread crumbs, season with pepper, drizzle with nice olive oil, and serve.

Chocolate Tart with Black and White Whipped Cream

Makes 1 (11-inch) tart

There is something really wonderful about whipped cream swirled with chocolate—it's like a soft-serve ice cream. It's great on this chocolate tart, but also on lots and lots of other things—it's even good stirred into hot coffee.

FOR THE CRUST

1 cup all-purpose flour

¼ cup sugar

Pinch of salt

½ cup (1 stick) butter, melted

1 teaspoon vanilla extract

FOR THE FILLING

12 ounces semisweet chocolate, chopped

½ cup (1 stick) butter

3 eggs

⅓ cup sugar

1 cup heavy cream

½ teaspoon salt

FOR THE BLACK AND WHITE WHIPPED CREAM

4 ounces good-quality dark chocolate (I like Mast Brothers),
    chopped

1 cup heavy cream

1 drop vanilla extract

Make the crust. Heat the oven to 350°F. Whisk the flour together with the sugar and salt. Stir in the melted butter and vanilla, then press the crust into the tart pan. Bake the shell until golden brown, about 15 minutes. Take the tart shell out of the oven but leave the oven on.

Make the filling while the crust is baking. Combine the semi-sweet chocolate and butter in a heatproof bowl set atop a pan of simmering water over low heat. Melt the chocolate, stirring constantly, then set the mixture aside to cool for 5 minutes.

Whisk the eggs together with the sugar in a large bowl until the mixture is pale yellow; whisk in the cream and salt. Whisk a little of the chocolate mixture into the egg mixture, then gradually whisk in the remaining chocolate.

Pour the filling into the tart shell (it is OK if it's not completely cool). Bake the tart until the edges of the filling puff and the center is almost but not quite set, 20 to 25 minutes. Take the tart out of the oven and allow it to cool.

Make the whipped cream. Melt the dark chocolate in a heatproof bowl set atop a pan of simmering water over low heat, stirring constantly, until it is smooth. Remove the bowl from the heat and allow it to cool for 10 minutes. Meanwhile, whisk the cream until soft peaks form. Add 1 drop of vanilla, whip a bit more, then quickly and gently fold the chocolate into the cream, just enough so it creates a nice swirl.

Slice the pie and serve topped with generous dollops of whipped cream.

WINTER MENU

Seafood salad

Crispy chicken

Kale gnocchi & ragu

Stuffed delicata

Hazelnut tart

KNIVES

Winter on Martha's Vineyard is a time to regroup and repair. It is an opportunity to get things in order — if not your life, at least your tools. In my case that includes my collection of much-used knives. I am attached to them — happy with my small cache, each exactly what I need.

You can spend a lot of money on knives. I don't. I want a knife I can depend on and don't have to worry about beating up. I buy cheaper knives because I've found they get the job done and are easier to maintain — they are made of slightly softer steel, so sharpening is less of a chore. I have friends, chefs and good cooks alike, who swear by their hand-forged Japanese beauties, but I think of my kitchen equipment in much the same way I think about most tools — best not too pretty, and ideally well broken in. As far as brands go, I've been happy with my Victorinox, Dexter, and E. Dehillerin knives.

You really need only a few knives — a chef's knife, a stiff boning knife, a flexible boning knife, and a paring knife. A chef's knife is where you can wind up spending the most money, but you can get a good one for as little as thirty-five dollars. I prefer a thinner blade. I find some of the well-known German models a little too bulky and hard to sharpen. A sharp paring knife is great for smaller jobs and detail work, peeling vegetables, slicing fruit, and dicing shallots. Working in a restaurant, paring knives tend to go missing, so my general inclination to buy cheap is strongest here: I tend to buy five at a time at about eight dollars each.

I use a stiff 6-inch boning knife to break down meat. You need the knife to be rigid enough to fight the tendons and sinew. The same knife is great for trimming vegetables and harvesting herbs. For boning and filleting, I rely on a 6-inch flexible boning knife. The flex allows me to follow the contours of carcasses, leaving them bare.

Knives dull quickly. The dullness is a consequence of two things — first, the "teeth" of the blade get out of alignment; and second, the angle of the edge becomes less pronounced. Straight-bladed knives actually have too-tiny-to-see teeth forged into the blades — like a serrated knife, just much, much smaller. Every time you use a knife these little teeth get banged around, so to keep your knife sharp you need to straighten them. This is done by honing with a kitchen steel. You should use your steel before you begin to cook and throughout your prep. I favor a flat model with a fine diamond grit. Buy a good one — I spent twice as much for my steel as for my chef's knife.

To truly sharpen a knife you need to redefine the blade and return the angle of the edge of the teeth to their original sharp intensity. For this you need a sharpening stone. There are two main types of stones, oil-lubricated (my grandfather used one) and water-lubricated (a slightly softer, more porous stone — which I use). There are synthetic and natural stones of both kinds. My preference is for a two-sided stone with a 1,000 grit on one side and 4,000 on the other. The lower grit is what I use to bring back a lost edge or define a new one. The higher grit is for finishing things up.

This is how I sharpen my knives: I soak my stone in water for 10 minutes. Then I set it on a damp towel on the counter, with the long side tracing the edge of the counter. The trick to sharpening is working your knife over the surface of the stone evenly with consistent pressure, so it's important to focus. I wipe my knife to remove any dust, then grip the handle firmly between my fingers and thumb with the blade facing away; I don't allow the handle to rest in my palm. I extend the fingers of my other hand out over the length of the blade, leaving my thumb pointed up and away. Now I press the blade edge onto the stone and begin sliding my knife toward me, starting at the base of the blade and working toward the tip, forming an arc, applying equal, even pressure to all sections as they pass over the stone. The angle against the stone is key. I generally go with an angle of almost 15 degrees, more severe than some recommendations, but this allows me a sharper bevel.

I slide the knife across the stone smoothly and evenly five times, then flip the knife over, trade my grip, and do five strokes on the other side of the blade. Then I repeat, working through five even strokes on each side two more times. That done, I flip the knife and begin counting down — passing the knife four times on one side then the other, then three times, then two, then one. This gives me an even edge. Do it the same way every time so your knife stays even. Finish up with a few swipes on the other side of the stone, then on your steel, and a wipe from your towel.

Of course if you are starting with a very dull knife, or one made of harder steel, you'll need to go at it longer. You can get your knives professionally sharpened, but be careful not to do this too often — most professional services grind knives, which will shorten the life of your knife. This is one of those chores that is worth doing yourself.

Seafood Salad

This salad is a celebration of whatever is best at the fish market. The number of ingredients is a function of what looks best and will fluctuate with the time of year—the list below is just a loose guide. If only the squid is perfect, limit yourself to that; same goes for the other ingredients. I present the salad differently depending on the occasion. For a formal meal I arrange the seafood individually over the dressed pea leaves. For a casual dinner, I combine it all in a bowl and dress everything together. Either way, I cook each item separately—the only way to treat the delicate seafood right.

½ pound squid tentacles (chopped if large)

About 2½ cups extra-virgin olive oil

2 cloves garlic, peeled

2 to 3 lemons, 1 quarter reserved; the rest juiced

Kosher salt

Pinch crushed red pepper

1 lobster, 1¼ pounds

2 cups white wine

16 mussels, beards removed

2½ cups loosely packed pea leaves (if you can't find pea leaves, substitute arugula)

½ cup loosely packed fresh parsley leaves

About 1 tablespoon neutral oil, such as canola oil

8 bay scallops (or 4 ounces sea scallops, cleaned and sliced)

Freshly ground black pepper

Poach the squid. Combine the squid and 2 cups of the olive oil in a small saucepan. Add the garlic cloves and lemon quarter. Season the oil with salt and red pepper and warm over medium heat. When small bubbles begin to appear, turn the heat down and let the squid poach gently in the oil until it is opaque and tender, about 1 hour (as the squid expresses liquid it will reduce in size by about two-thirds). Allow the squid to cool in the oil, then refrigerate it.

Cook the lobster. Bring a pot of salted water to a boil over high heat. Add the lobster, cover, and boil for 5 minutes. Drain the lobster, let cool slightly, then remove the meat from the shells. Chunk the lobster meat, then dress lightly with about 3 tablespoons olive oil, about 2 tablespoons lemon juice, and salt. Refrigerate until you are ready to make the salad.

Cook the mussels. Heat up a large saucepan over high heat. Add the wine. When it's boiling vigorously, add the mussels. Cover and cook until the mussels open, about 3 minutes. Transfer the mussels to a bowl. Remove them from their shells and refrigerate until ready to finish the salad.

Make the pea leaf dressing. Bring a pot of salted water to a boil. Add 1½ cups of the pea leaves and blanch until the leaves are bright green. Drain and refresh in ice water. Drain and transfer to a food processor. Add the parsley leaves and neutral oil and pulse until the dressing is smooth. Season with salt. Taste and adjust the consistency if necessary by adding a bit more neutral oil or a little water. Reserve.

Cook the scallops. Put the scallops in a small pot and add water to cover. Season the water with lots of salt—it should taste like the ocean. Bring to a simmer, reduce the heat, and poach the scallops at just below a simmer, cooking them until they are opaque but not yet firm, about 4 minutes. Remove the scallops from the water and put in a bowl. Dress them with about 3 tablespoons olive oil, about 2 tablespoons lemon juice, and black pepper. Refrigerate until you are ready to assemble the salad.

To finish the salad, pull all the seafood out of the refrigerator. Put the mussels in a bowl and dress with a little of the pea leaf dressing. Taste the lobster and scallops and adjust the seasoning with salt, olive oil, and lemon juice as needed. Drain the squid (discard the oil or keep it to poach more squid—it will last weeks in the refrigerator).

Arrange the remaining 1 cup pea leaves on plates and season with salt. Arrange each type of seafood on the plates, one at a time. Alternatively, combine the pea leaves and seafood in a bowl and mix gently, seasoning to taste with salt and lemon juice. Either way, thin the remaining pea leaf dressing with a tablespoon or so of lemon juice. Drizzle over the salads, finish with additional olive oil if desired, and serve.

Crispy Chicken

Serves 4

On the one hand, this is a simple recipe, on the other, it takes some practice to get it exactly right, so I am going to go into extra detail below. Don't be daunted—you'll be happy I did. The chicken winds up perfectly juicy with crispy skin. I suggest you buy whole farm-raised birds, because they really do taste better. This recipe is for the legs and thighs only. For some thoughts about what to do with breasts, liver, and bones, see pages 139–140.

> 4 whole chicken legs (with thighs), boned (see Note on next page)
> Kosher salt
> About 2 tablespoons neutral oil, such as canola
> 1 lemon

Remove the chicken from the refrigerator and pat it dry. Liberally salt the skin side. Don't salt the flesh. Heat a large skillet over high heat. Add a coating of oil. When the oil is hot and easily slides across the pan, pour off

any excess. Add the chicken, skin-side down, and pull the pan off the heat for a minute or so to let the skin render some.

When the sizzling becomes gentler, return the skillet to the heat—turned down to medium-low. Cook the chicken at a constant low sizzle, giving the pan a shake after a couple of minutes to loosen the chicken from the pan. Continue cooking, moving the chicken around a bit now and then to bring more of the surface in contact with the heat of the pan, rendering the skin and maintaining a constant moderately low sizzle. Cook this way, turning the flame up or down as necessary, until the skin is evenly golden, at least 20 minutes from the time the chicken went into the pan. Now turn up the heat to medium-high and finish crisping the skin, about another 4 minutes, moving the chicken often.

Flip the chicken and cook it for a minute or two on the second side, until it is just cooked through. Pull the pan off the heat and let the chicken rest in the skillet for 5 minutes. Transfer the chicken to a cutting board, slice, and serve with a wedge of lemon, a drizzle of pan juices, and a final sprinkle of sea salt.

Note: To bone the chicken legs, start by making an incision along the thighbone. Run your knife around the bone to free the meat from it. Ignore the joint for the moment and make a cut through the "ankle," then cut through the tendons. Then cut up along the bone, back toward the joint between the thigh and lower leg. Cut around the leg bone, freeing the meat. Cut away the leg and thighbones and reserve for stock. Now, carefully work your knife under the "knee" cartilage, trying not to pierce the skin—but don't worry if you do, the chicken will be a little less pretty but equally delicious. If you aren't up to boning the legs yourself, ask your butcher. I use the same method to cook boneless thighs.

CHICKEN PARTS

SALT-BAKED CHICKEN BREASTS

Baking boneless, skinless chicken breasts surrounded by salt is a remarkably effective way to keep them moist while concentrating their flavor. For 2 medium breasts, put 4 cups kosher salt in a bowl. Mix in enough water, about ½ cup, so the salt is the consistency of wet beach sand. Put some herbs and aromatics in the salt mixture—a few sprigs of rosemary and several strips of lemon zest are nice. Put a ½-inch layer of the salt mixture in a pan or baking dish big enough to hold the chicken in a single layer. Lay the boneless, skinless chicken breasts on the salt, then cover them with the remaining salt mixture, packing it so you have about ½ inch all around. Bake the chicken in a 400°F oven for 15 minutes. Take them out of the oven and let them rest for 5 to 10 minutes. Brush off the salt and slice. Serve warm or chilled with Radish Salsa Verde (variation of Salsa Verde, page 260).

CHICKEN LIVERS

Chicken livers are a great place to start a crostini or sandwich. For this recipe you will need 5 livers. I recommend you freeze chicken livers, stockpiling them from birds until you get enough, or, of course, you can simply buy 4 additional livers from a butcher. Dice an onion, then sweat it in a skim of canola oil in a skillet over medium heat until soft and golden, about 15 minutes. Transfer to a food processor. Add a little more oil to the skillet, raise the heat, and sauté the chicken livers until they are firm, about 1 minute per side. Put the livers in the processor with the onions. While the pan is hot, deglaze it with ½ tablespoon bourbon. Cook it for a minute or so, then add this to the processor. Season the liver mixture with salt and pepper, then pulse in room temperature butter, a tablespoon at a time, until the mixture is smooth, about 12 tablespoons butter in all. Add a tablespoon of apple cider vinegar and adjust the seasoning with salt and pepper. Refrigerate until ready to serve. Makes about 1 cup.

CHICKEN STOCK

One of the ancillary benefits of buying whole chickens is a freezer full of stock. You can start with a raw carcass, bones, and wings after taking the legs for Crispy Chicken, page 137, or start with the browned bones from a roast. My basic approach is the same in both cases: I put the raw or roasted bones in a pot and add water to cover by a couple of inches. Sometimes I add aromatics — coarsely chopped onion, carrot, and celery — and sometimes I keep things simple. Either way, I bring the water to a boil, then reduce the heat to a simmer and cook, skimming away froth and fat, until the stock tastes chickeny — about 1 hour. Then I let it cool, strain it, and stow it in quart containers in my freezer. Depending on what you start with and how far you let things reduce, you can expect that a medium bird will yield 2 or more quarts of stock.

Kale Gnocchi with Kale Ragu

Serves 4 as a first course or side dish

This is a vegetarian riff on pasta with a hearty, meaty ragu. It works as a first course, side dish, or main. I've given kale a moment to shine, using it both in the gnocchi—a more substantial alternative to wheat pasta—and in the deeply flavored sauce. Use young kale leaves if you can find them, you can sliver the whole leaf, stem included. If you use large leaves, you'll need to trim the stems as they can be tough. Buy enough extra so you wind up with 1 pound of trimmed leaves. I like to make the gnocchi ahead, parboil, and then reheat them just before serving. But you can make them just before serving—this eliminates the need to reheat them before you add them to the sauce, but you'll need to get it going while you cook the potatoes.

FOR THE GNOCCHI

2 pounds russet potatoes (2 medium)

Kosher salt

½ pound Tuscan young kale, thinly slivered

1 cup all-purpose flour

1 egg

FOR THE KALE RAGU

¼ cup extra-virgin olive oil

1 small onion, minced

½ small fennel bulb, trimmed and minced

1 stalk celery, trimmed and minced

Kosher salt

Pinch crushed red pepper

½ pound young Tuscan kale, thinly slivered

Freshly grated Parmigiano-Reggiano

Make the gnocchi. Place the potatoes in a pot and cover with water. Add salt and bring to a boil over high heat. Reduce the heat and simmer until the potatoes are easily pierced with a knife, about 1 hour in total. Heat the oven to 300°F when the potatoes are almost done.

Blanch the kale while the potatoes cook. Bring a large pot of salted water to a boil over high heat. Add the slivered kale and cook until tender, about 3 minutes for young kale and 7 minutes for mature leaves. Drain the kale, refresh in ice water, then finely chop. Wrap the chopped kale in a clean kitchen towel and squeeze out as much liquid as you can (squeeze hard—if your kale is too wet your gnocchi will be soggy and heavy).

Drain the potatoes and put them in the oven, directly on the rack, to dry out. Bake until they no longer steam when squeezed, about 25 minutes. While the potatoes are still hot (hold them with a towel), peel and then put through a ricer (alternatively, you can very quickly grate them).

Spread the potatoes out on a clean work surface. Sprinkle the chopped steamed kale on the potatoes. Mound the flour next to the potatoes. Make a well in the mound and add a pinch of salt and the egg. Mix the egg with your fingers, then, working quickly, incorporate it into the flour. When the egg is distributed, begin working in the warm potatoes, gathering the dough with your hands until it is just smooth (take care not to over-handle the dough). Gather the dough into a ball; if it is still sticky, dust it with flour.

Cut the dough in quarters. Roll each portion into a log about ¾ inch thick. Cut the logs into small gnocchi (about 1 inch or so). Dust the gnocchi with flour to prevent sticking and cover with a clean kitchen towel.

Parboil the gnocchi. Bring a large pot of salted water to a boil over high heat. Set up an ice bath. Working in batches, parboil the gnocchi in the boiling water until they float. Retrieve them with a slotted spoon, and refresh in your ice bath. When all the gnocchi are cooked, refreshed, and drained, coat them lightly with oil. Keep in a covered container in the refrigerator (for up to 2 days).

Start the ragu by making the soffritto. Heat the oil in a large, deep skillet over medium heat. Add the onion, fennel, and celery. Season with salt and cook, stirring frequently, until the vegetables are lightly golden, about 30 minutes. (As the vegetables cook they will release their juices and shrink by about a third; stir more often as they begin to color to prevent them from burning.)

Add the red pepper and kale, stir well, and reduce the heat to low. Add a couple of tablespoons of water, cover, and cook until the kale is tender, about 20 minutes. Adjust the seasoning with salt.

Reheat the gnocchi and assemble the dish. Bring a pot of salted water to a boil over high heat. Reheat the gnocchi by dropping them briefly in the boiling water. Drain them, then add to the ragu, along with enough pasta water to loosen the sauce. Increase the heat briefly so the flavors combine, then serve topped with Parmigiano-Reggiano.

Stuffed Delicata Squash

Serves 4

Delicata squash is harvested early in the fall but keeps until spring. Unlike most winter squash varieties, the skin of a delicata is thin and delicious. I like to highlight this by spooning seasoned mashed squash into the roasted skin-on "shells."

4 delicata squash, halved lengthwise, pulp and seeds removed

Kosher salt

About 2 tablespoons neutral oil, such as canola, plus additional for frying the rosemary

3 cloves garlic, unpeeled

1 tablespoon rosemary leaves

Heat the oven to 425°F. Place a large metal or ceramic baking dish in the oven to preheat (the baking dish should be big enough to hold all the squash halves in a single layer; if the dish is too small, use two).

Season the squash with salt. Add the oil, a generous coating, to the hot baking dish. Add the garlic, then the squash, cut-side down. Roast the squash, basting every 5 minutes with the oil in the pan, until the cut sides are nicely browned, 10 to 15 minutes. Check the garlic as you baste, removing it when it is soft, about 8 minutes. Turn the squash halves over and continue roasting, basting occasionally, until it is tender, about 10 minutes more.

While the squash is roasting, fry the rosemary leaves. Heat a small saucepan over high heat. Add about ½ inch of oil. When the oil begins to smoke, add the rosemary and fry, moving it so it browns and crisps evenly, about 2 minutes. Carefully drain the rosemary (set a strainer over a heat-proof bowl). Allow the rosemary and oil to cool. Reserve the oil for another use (I use it to baste lean cuts of meat).

Scoop the flesh from 4 of the squash halves into a mixing bowl. Add the fried rosemary, then peel and mash the roasted garlic and add that. Mix thoroughly; season with salt.

Spoon the seasoned squash mash into the remaining roasted halves and serve.

TOASTED SEEDS

Like all squash and pumpkin seeds, delicata seeds are good toasted. Blanch the seeds and pulp in boiling water until the water returns to a boil, stirring the water aggressively to separate one seed from another. Drain the seeds and discard the pulp. Dry the seeds and put them on a baking sheet in a single layer. Lightly oil and salt, then bake at 300°F until they are fragrant and golden, about 1 hour. Cool and store in an airtight container.

Chocolate Hazelnut Torte

Makes 1 (9-inch) cake

This cake is light and airy—a chocolate dessert that isn't at all heavy (and it's gluten-free). I serve it with whipped cream and toasted hazelnuts.

  1 cup hazelnuts

  8 ounces bittersweet or semi-sweet chocolate, chopped then chilled

  1 cup sugar

  1 cup egg whites (about 8 eggs)

  ¼ teaspoon cream of tartar

Heat the oven to 325°F. Generously grease a 9-inch springform pan.

Spread the hazelnuts on a baking sheet and toast in the oven until they smell nutty and the skins can be easily rubbed off, about 8 minutes. Place the toasted nuts in a folded kitchen towel and gently rub to remove their skins, then refrigerate the cleaned hazelnuts for 10 minutes to cool.

Combine the nuts, chocolate, and ½ cup of the sugar in a food processor. Pulse until the mixture is the texture of coarse meal.

In a mixer using the whisk attachment or by hand, whip the egg whites with the cream of tartar until the whites foam. Whisking continuously, gradually add the remaining ½ cup of sugar, beating into shiny, soft peaks. Fold half the nut mixture into the whites, then repeat.

Spoon the batter into the pan and smooth with a spatula. Bake until the cake is golden brown and puffed, about 35 minutes. Allow the cake to cool for 10 minutes, then unmold and allow it to cool completely before slicing and serving.

SIGNS of SPRING

marinated anchovy and island egg crostino

salted bass, savoy cabbage, and polenta

oysters roasted over coals
flank steak hammered thin

maple ice cream and ginger cookies

CROSTINI

The combination of empty or uninspiring grocery shelves and a full freezer — the usual wintertime state of things around here — can lead a cook toward a routine, a rotation of dishes you like and know how to make, that you can plan for. Or you can let it push you. I like to try for make-do creativity. Recently my creations tend to balance on a piece of bread. I love crostini, "little toasts" — which are really small open-faced sandwiches. Crostini are sometimes simple, often rustic, and occasionally truly elegant. They are my go-to answer to the question of how to start a meal with friends in February as well as what I most like to eat when I am by myself.

Because you are only dealing with a single slice of bread, the topping gets to shine. But the bread is important too. Toasted or grilled it is my starting point — but not always the hero of my effort. I did not grow up eating good bread — it just wasn't available here. I ate my scrambled eggs and my tomato-and-mayonnaise sandwiches on thin slices of white toast — which I still like. My thinking on sandwich bread is that it has its place, and it is best with something really good on top — but you have to keep things in balance. You need your topping to be delicious, but you also want it to be a little demure. Asparagus on Toast with *gribiche* (page 210) fills the bill. The combination of delicate asparagus, creamy soft-cooked egg, and crunchy pickled carrots on nicely toasted white toast works magically.

I first started eating "good bread" when I moved to New York. I remember using any excuse I could to stop in at Jim Lahey's Sullivan Street Bakery, then a few blocks from my apartment. His loaves, inspired by Roman bread I would encounter a few years later, were a wonderful combination of light and airy, slightly soured and toothsome. His no-knead recipe, detailed in his book, *My Bread: The Revolutionary No-Work, No-Knead Method*, is an excellent place to begin if you are planning to make your own.

For crostini, when you start with a beautiful piece of chewy sourdough with a good hard crust, you are ahead of the game. You can be as simple or creative as you want. Toast the bread, season it with a little salt, pour on your best olive oil, and call it a day. Or rub it with a garlic clove and call it *fettunta* — like the Italians. Or get just a little bit more fancy: Top the bread with a little oil and add an ingredient you love — great prosciutto or sautéed kale or an oozy cheese. Or try

going one step further and layer flavors and textures to create a complex but balanced bite—or two or three.

Some ideas to keep in mind when you start to elaborate:

- Creamy is good. I top both simple and more complicated crostini with Chicken Livers (see page 140); soft-cooked egg; rich, spreadable, or crumbly cheese; or pureed beans or vegetables—even pureed salami.
- Balance as you go. Offset richness with acid and tang—lemon and vinegar bring excitement to things. Layer salty or peppery elements with blander flavors. Cured pork of all kinds is great. So are anchovies.
- Vegetables are nice fresh but also cooked. Try tomatoes, lightly dressed greens, and radishes raw; peppers roasted; carrots, beets, or cauliflower pickled; or cauliflower sautéed. Mix it up.
- Don't forget about seafood! Clams and mussels and lobster are all terrific on toasted bread, and the cooking juices left in the pan are the perfect "sauce," they are meant to be sopped up.
- Pile it high, keep it interesting, but remember to edit. Get inspired by flavor combinations you like in other dishes but don't be afraid to experiment, and always serve all but the simplest crostini with a knife and fork.

Egg and Anchovy Crostini

Serves 4

The anchovies I use here are marinated. They taste more like herring than the salted fillets available at the supermarket. Look for them at high-end groceries with fish markets.

> 4 eggs
>
> Kosher salt
>
> 1 cup loosely packed baby sorrel or other tender green, chopped
>
> Good extra-virgin olive oil
>
> Country bread or baguette, sliced and toasted (I like to cut baguettes lengthwise, then cut each half into pieces for chewier, more substantial "toast")
>
> 4 to 8 marinated white anchovy fillets
>
> Freshly ground black pepper

Bring a pot of salted water to a boil over high heat. Put the eggs in the water and let them cook for 6 minutes. Drain, rinse under cold water, then peel. Refrigerate for at least 20 minutes to allow the yolks to set.

Break (or cut) the eggs in half and sprinkle with salt. Dress the baby sorrel with a little olive oil and season lightly with salt. Put the sorrel on the bread and top with an egg and an anchovy fillet (or two). Season with pepper, drizzle with olive oil, and serve.

Polenta with Salted Fish and Cabbage

Serves 4

Salted fish is the perfect accompaniment to creamy polenta, a winter staple for me. But remember to allow two days to soak the fish — just in case.

4 ounces salted bass or cod (see Salting Fish, page 98)

½ cup medium-grind polenta (I like Alpina Savoie)

Kosher salt

½ small head savoy cabbage, outer leaves and core removed

About 2 tablespoons extra-virgin olive oil

¼ cup milk

2 tablespoons butter

¼ cup loosely packed fresh parsley leaves, chopped

To rehydrate the fish, put it in a bowl, add water to cover, and seal with plastic wrap. Refrigerate for 12 hours, changing the water twice. Taste a little piece. If it tastes lightly salted, not salty, then drain it. If not, change the water and continue soaking the fillets.

Bring 3½ cups water to a boil in a medium saucepan over high heat. Whisk in the polenta in a slow, steady stream. Stir until the polenta returns to a boil, then reduce the heat to low. Add a little salt and cook, stirring often, until the polenta tastes smooth, about 1 hour.

While the polenta cooks, roast the cabbage. Heat the oven to 400°F. Cut the cabbage into quarters. Put the cabbage wedges in a bowl, season with salt, and coat with a little oil. Transfer to a baking sheet and roast, turning the wedges several times, until they are golden and tender, about 15 minutes.

Drain the fish and cut it into small pieces. Stir the fish, milk, butter, and parsley into the polenta and cook until the fish is tender, about 5 minutes. Taste and adjust the seasoning with salt if necessary. Arrange the cabbage wedges in 4 shallow bowls. Spoon the polenta over the cabbage and serve.

Pounded Flank Steak with
Coal-Roasted Oysters

Serves 4

Last winter my dad left me a bucket of oysters. I roasted them with butter and they added a nice richness to the lean, pounded flank steak I had defrosted (cut from one of my cousin's cows). You could cook the steak on the grill and the oysters in the coals, but last March the weather was so dreary and cold we preferred to stay inside. I cooked the steak on the stove and roasted the oysters in the fireplace and it was just fine.

1 flank steak, about 1¼ pounds

Kosher salt

Freshly ground black pepper

2 tablespoons extra-virgin olive oil

4 tablespoons (½ stick) butter

1 shallot, sliced

2 small cloves garlic, sliced

1 teaspoon red wine vinegar

12 oysters, on the half-shell

Season the steak liberally with salt, then pound with a meat cleaver until ¼ to ½ inch thick. Season well with pepper. Heat a large skillet over high heat. Add the oil, then sear the steak until it is browned on both sides, about 1½ minutes per side for medium-rare (my preference). Transfer the steak to a cutting board to rest for a few minutes. Slice the steak against the grain on a slight bias, put on a platter, and hold in a warm place.

Melt 3 tablespoons of the butter in a small skillet over medium heat. Add the shallots and garlic and let soften for about 3 minutes. Swirl in the remaining 1 tablespoon of cold butter and the vinegar.

Place the oysters in hot coals, fireplace embers, or under a hot broiler. When they begin to bubble and firm up, 1 to 2 minutes, pull them out of the heat. Spoon the butter sauce over the oysters and serve with the steak.

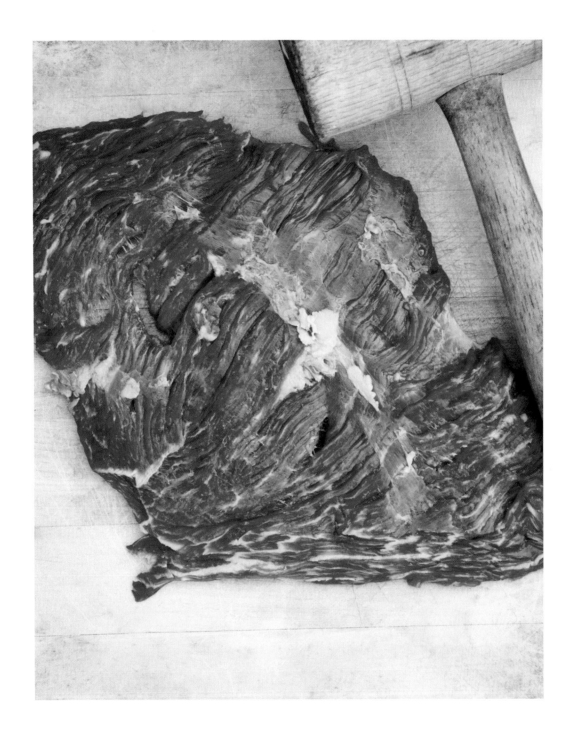

OYSTERING

I went to see Johnny because he doesn't answer his phone. I went on a Sunday when the weather was ugly — figuring he'd be home. I bumped along the rutted road under angry skies to his house until I got to his yard, busy with scrap wood, split logs, boats, chickens, anvils, cinderblocks, buoys, coiled rope, tractors (one yellow and one red), leftover stone, and some scaffolding — an assortment of mismatched clutter, but all useful. That is why it was there.

I found Johnny at his desk. His open computer was sitting on a stack of unsorted, weeks-old mail next to an open Cabela's catalog. An electric glove-dryer shaped like hands sported a well-used orange pair at the corner of the desk. As we talked schedule, Johnny checked the forecast and his gloves.

Tomorrow, he said, looked like a good day to go out in the boat, the weather was supposed to clear and he could bring his son. The oysters, he noted, would be better now that the "cut" from the ocean to the Great Pond was open again. Johnny would know. The brackish winter-grey water of the pond weaves through his property. The spindly salt-stunted oak trees hide it from sight, but you can feel it close by.

He was young, in his twenties, when he and a friend started hearing rumors that the Japanese were paying top dollar for wild oysters — with a premium on really big ones. Johnny considered various angles, then remembered the defunct Great Pond oyster farm the Mayhews ran in the fifties and sixties — they called it the Quansoo Shellfish Company. Johnny and his friend guessed that since nobody had bothered with it for years, the pond bottom was probably covered with massive oysters. All they needed was a boat. "It took us six hours, plywood, basement tar for bottom paint," he told me,

> and before you knew it we were seaworthy and
> leaving an oil slick in our wake because we
> didn't have time for the paint to dry. Chris and
> I would go. My wife Barbara had a permit as
> well. We were allowed ten bushels a week, and
> there were three of us, so we managed thirty
> bushels. We made $1,500; that was real money
> then and it's real money now. Only took us six
> hours to get our limit. Some of the oysters
> were as big as my shoe.

Johnny has worked the pond ever since; he's in his sixties now. He monitors the flavor of his catch throughout the year, snacking on broken-shelled specimens that it would be a shame to waste. If you ask Johnny, the best time of the year for oysters here is the fall, just after the cut is re-opened in October. The salt water rushes into the pond and seasons the oysters just enough to wake their flavor. In March the cracked oysters we slurp taste more vegetal and almost mushroom-like. They taste of the grasses and leaves that bound the streams that flow into the Great Pond. But I have to say, the early spring oysters taste briny, and luscious to me.

Maple Crème Fraîche Ice Cream

Makes about 1 quart

It is easy to make your own crème fraîche: Combine 2 cups heavy cream with ¼ cup buttermilk in a bowl. Cover with a towel and set aside at room temperature until thick, 24 to 48 hours; refrigerate until you are ready to use.

1 cup maple syrup

3 egg yolks

½ cup milk

2 cups crème fraîche (homemade or store-bought)

Mix ¼ cup of the maple syrup with the egg yolks in a bowl and set aside. Put the remaining ¾ cup syrup in a small saucepan. Bring it to a boil over medium-high heat, then allow it to reduce by a quarter, about 7 minutes. Take the pan off the heat and allow the mixture to cool for 5 minutes.

Gradually stir the milk into the reduced syrup. Temper the egg mixture by whisking in a little of the milk mixture then gradually whisking in the rest. Put the ice cream base in the saucepan and heat over medium, whisking and then stirring with a wooden spoon, until the mixture thickens enough to coat the spoon (if you have a candy thermometer you want it to get to 160°F). Remove the ice cream base from the heat and let it cool for 5 minutes.

Put the crème fraîche in a bowl. Gradually whisk the ice cream base into the crème fraîche; cover and chill for at least 2 hours.

Process the ice cream in an ice cream maker according to the manufacturer's instructions. Serve immediately or pack into containers and store in the freezer.

DINNER

 ON THE PASTURE
BY THE SEA

A CABBAGE SALAD

ROPE GROWN MUSSELS

SPRING LAMB SHANKS

AND HONEY PIE

A WEDDING TO REMEMBER

The broad fields push right up to the marshes on the far side of the Great Pond. The Atlantic is right there too, salting the meadows with spray. It is a beautiful setting, but the Allen Farm's stunning location has practical value — the sea air gives the grazing sheep a deep-seasoned flavor that could only come from these fields. Mitchell Posin and his son, Ned, work their farm together and they are a good duo, raising their sheep carefully, walking in all weather, broad-shouldered and strong, their curly heads bent toward one another, tending to the flock by caring for their grass.

Mitchell will tell you that it all starts by paying attention to the micro-biology of the soil. He looks and acts like he was born on the farm, but he began life in the city, in hard-scrabble Brooklyn. It is his wife, Clarissa Allen, who has lived more or less always on the hundred acres of Chilmark pastureland that have been in her family since 1762. She left the island and thought she would settle in Boston or maybe New York, but when her parents died, Clarissa, an only child, inherited the property. (The Allens, in stark contrast to my large-brooded ancestors, have typically had small families, which makes it simpler to keep property intact. Ned, like his mother, is an only child.)

Clarissa and Mitchell met and fell in love. It was meant to be. She had a large run-down farm she loved but didn't quite know what to do with and he was a born farmer — he just hadn't started yet. They moved into the three-hundred-year-old house, eventually rebuilding it while they revitalized the overgrown pastures, clearing them with grazing goats until grass could grow plentifully and sheep could once again make a home on the Allen Farm.

They raise the best lamb I've ever tasted; it is what I want to eat and serve in damp and blustery March and April. I can taste it in my imagination and the memory brings my thoughts shooting back to Ned's truly magnificent wedding. It was this past October, when the Allen Farm's fields were put to special use. That is where Ned married his high-school sweetheart. The wedding was a big event, with 450 guests invited. The plan, many months in the making, was that Mitchell would provide all the meat and I would organize cooking it. Guests would make side dishes.

The sheep, calves, pigs, and chickens were slaughtered over the course of weeks leading up to the big day. I made sure I was present when Fernando, whom Mitchell trusts to kill his animals, did his work. It was remarkable to watch him stroke and whisper to each animal, stilling it before moving it from this world to the next. Mitchell supervised, organized equipment, and helped with the hanging and skinning. Clarissa brought steaming coffee and tea to the barn from the house, stepping lightly over pools of blood and piles of knives. I can still picture Ned smiling through the acrid smoke that shadowed his face as he burnt the hair from the swine with a blowtorch.

We built our fires in the field overlooking the ocean across the road from the house. We cooked those pigs in two enormous smokers for 24 hours, taking turns tending overnight. We roasted hot dogs over the firebox and ate them sitting in lawn chairs under umbrellas, shielded from passing showers, through the night. In the morning we dashed to the ocean to rinse off before getting back to work.

The chickens were skewered and the beef portioned and grilled. The lambs roasted upright, splayed on Argentine-style contraptions (which looked like crucifixes) designed and constructed for the occasion by a neighbor. Everything was cooked over oak Ned had harvested and split. A stream of friends stopped by; some had planned to, others were attracted by the spectacle—the unaccustomed activity in the roadside pastures, the smoke, and the sense that something momentous was going on.

That afternoon, as the light faded, the vows were spoken. Lines of carvers organized near the quieting fires, then platters were loaded and carried on laps bumping across the field in a truck to the tents. The guests ate their meat with applesauce Mitchell made from apples he'd picked at dawn. He'd carried it down from the house in 5-gallon buckets that he'd hastily labeled just before he put on his suit.

Grilled Cabbage Salad with Ricotta Salata and Ground Cherries

Serves 4

Although you will miss a bit of smoky flavor, you can cook both the cabbage and cheese in a dry, hot, cast-iron pan on the stovetop instead of on the grill. It takes a couple of extra minutes to get nicely caramelized, but the results are good. If you can't find tart, fruity ground cherries (also known as husk tomatoes), this salad is also nice made with toasted hazelnuts and cherry tomatoes.

> 3 ounces ricotta salata
>
> About 4 tablespoons neutral oil, such as canola oil
>
> Kosher salt
>
> About 4 tablespoons extra-virgin olive oil
>
> 1 lemon
>
> ½ teaspoon fresh marjoram leaves
>
> 1 medium to large head savoy cabbage
>
> ½ cup peeled ground cherries
>
> 1 cup loosely packed small or torn mint leaves
>
> ½ cup sliced almonds, lightly toasted

Grill the cheese. Heat a grill over high heat. Cut the cheese into three thick, even slices and rub each with neutral oil and a little salt. Grill to mark on each side, about 20 seconds per side. Place the cheese in a bowl, then pour a tablespoon of each of the oils over it to marinate. Peel the rind from a quarter of the lemon. Finely chop the rind with a pinch of salt and add it to the bowl along with a squeeze of lemon juice. Add the marjoram leaves and mix with a spoon, crumbling the cheese as you go. Taste the marinated cheese and adjust the seasoning with both oils, lemon juice, and salt if needed. Set aside so the flavors blend. Keep the grill hot for the cabbage.

Pull off 15 large outer leaves of cabbage (give them a rinse if they seem gritty; then dry them). Set the leaves aside. Cut out the core and discard, then cut the remaining cabbage into wedges and separate the leaves. Reserve in a large bowl.

Grill the reserved outer cabbage leaves. Working in batches, place them, dry, on an oiled grill, curved-side up, so the edges lie on the grill and the centers bow a little. Grill until the edges brown and the leaves relax, but the ribs are still a little toothsome, about 2 minutes. Remove and reserve.

Prepare the raw cabbage salad. Dress the uncooked cabbage wedges with lemon juice, a tablespoon each of both oils, and some salt. Using your fingers, rub the dressing into the leaves. Add a little more of each oil and some salt and continue working the dressing into the bruised cabbage. Add half the ground cherries, tossing them with the salad. Take 3 of the grilled leaves and tear them into the bowl. Add the mint and half of the cheese and toss lightly. Adjust the seasoning if necessary with more lemon, salt, and olive oil, and then add the remaining ground cherries.

To serve, place 3 grilled leaves on each plate. Mound salad on the grilled leaves, dress with the toasted almonds and remaining cheese, and serve.

Mussels with Parsley and Garlic

Serves 4

I met Al Gale in the nineties when we were in high school. We washed dishes together at The Feast of Chilmark (a long-gone restaurant located in the spot where my grandparents met). We called him "Hurricane Al," and he and I liked the job for the free food. These days Al fishes and farms seafood. Lately he's been rope-growing mussels — the best around. Higher prices for oysters have led some mussel growers to switch over. I will count myself lucky if Al bucks the market and sticks with it.

1 cup loosely packed fresh parsley leaves

6 dozen mussels, beards removed

About 1 tablespoon extra-virgin olive oil

1 clove garlic, minced

Pinch crushed red pepper

Kosher salt

Country bread or baguette, sliced and toasted if desired, for serving

Fill a small pot with water and bring to a boil over high heat. Add the parsley and blanch until it is bright green, about 1 minute. Drain and refresh in cold water. Puree in a blender with 1 cup water; reserve.

Put the mussels in a large pot. Add 1 cup of water, cover, and cook over high heat until the mussels open. Remove the pan from the heat, add the parsley puree, and stir to distribute.

Heat a skim of oil in a small skillet over medium-high heat. Add the garlic and crushed pepper. Toast the garlic, shaking the pan, until fragrant, 1 to 2 minutes. Season the garlic with salt and add it to the mussels. Stir, then spoon into bowls and serve with good bread.

Slow-Roasted Lamb Shanks with Parsnips

Serves 4

I like to marinate lamb shanks overnight. I prefer to use fore-shanks from a young animal—they are a little smaller and each is a perfect serving size. This marinade recipe is something to remember: I put the same ingredients in a blender and puree them and make a sauce that's ideal with grilled or roasted meat, and also nice as a dressing for spring vegetables.

FOR THE MARINADE

1½ cups yogurt

2 tablespoons extra-virgin olive oil

1 lemon peel, pith removed, cut into strips

1½ teaspoons dried mint

1 small red onion, sliced

4 slices Pickled Onions (page 282), optional

2 tablespoons of the onion pickling liquid; or 1 tablespoon white wine vinegar, 1 tablespoon fresh lemon juice, and 6 toasted coriander seeds

FOR THE LAMB AND PARSNIPS

4 small lamb shanks

Kosher salt

Freshly ground black pepper

4 medium parsnips, peeled, trimmed, and cut into crescents or rounds (all about the same size)

Prepare the marinade. In a large bowl, combine all the marinade ingredients and stir to mix.

Marinate the lamb. Season the shanks with salt and pepper. Add to the marinade and coat evenly. Cover the bowl and marinate in the refrigerator overnight.

Roast the lamb. Let the lamb come up to room temperature. Heat the oven to 250°F.

Transfer the lamb and marinade to a flameproof baking dish or ovenproof skillet big enough to hold the shanks in a snug single layer. Roast the lamb until the first sides are browned, about 3 hours. Turn the shanks and roast until the second sides are also brown, about 1 more hour. Remove the pan from the oven, cover, and let the shanks rest for about 20 minutes. (The lamb can be cooked several hours — even a day — ahead and refrigerated. To serve, reheat in a 300°F oven for about 30 minutes.)

Parboil the parsnips. Bring a large pot of salted water to a boil. Add the parsnips and cook until they are just tender, about 6 minutes, depending on how thickly you've cut them. Drain. (The parsnips can be parboiled ahead and finished just before serving.)

To serve, transfer the shanks to a serving platter. Place the roasting pan over medium-high heat and heat the pan juices. Add the parsnips to the pan and brown, turning frequently but gently, about 5 minutes. Spoon the parsnips onto the platter with the lamb and serve.

Olivia's Honey Pie

Makes 1 (10-inch) pie

Olivia is a self-taught baker who makes desserts I love. We both wanted to do something with the honey that Poppy's friend Andy collects from hives underneath the chestnut tree at Beetlebung, so Olivia came up with this delicious treat, inspired by *Toscapaj,* a Swedish caramel pie.

FOR THE CRUST

1 cup all-purpose flour

¼ cup sugar

¼ teaspoon salt

1 teaspoon vanilla extract

½ cup (1 stick) butter, melted then cooled

FOR THE FILLING

⅔ cup honey

1 tablespoon sugar

½ cup (1 stick) butter

1 small egg (if you only have a large egg, beat it then discard a scant tablespoon)

½ cup heavy cream

½ cup chopped almonds, lightly toasted

Heat the oven to 325°F.

Make the crust. Combine the flour, sugar, and salt in a large bowl and whisk to combine. Using a wooden spoon, stir in the vanilla extract and melted butter. Form the dough into a ball, then press into a 10-inch tart shell. Bake the crust (it is not necessary to weight it) until golden, about 15 minutes. Allow the crust to cool.

Make the filling. Combine the honey, sugar, and butter in a saucepan and heat over medium until the butter and sugar melt. Simmer the mixture until it darkens and reduces slightly, about 10 minutes. Let cool for at least 15 minutes.

When the honey mixture is cool, whisk in the egg and cream.

Scatter the almonds over the bottom of the tart shell and then top with the honey filling. Bake the tart until the filling is set and a rich amber, about 30 minutes. Cool, slice, and serve.

Welcome

a tart rhubarb
cocktail

potted duck

rich pea greens

good chicken

a rhubarb tart

A STRANGE BIRD

My most improbably famous relative, Nancy Luce, was born in West Tisbury in 1814. She was a sharp, vigorous young girl born into the largest family on the island at a time when Martha's Vineyard's economy was thriving. The whaling industry boomed. Ships left Edgartown Harbor reportedly fifty at a time. It was an exciting time to be an islander. But Nancy's life took an unfortunate turn.

It is not clear whether it was disease, accident, or genetic defect, but Nancy wound up peculiar. She lived most of her adult life alone, alienated from her family and ridiculed by her neighbors. Nancy's only solace was her chickens. She treated them like friends, christening them with names she concocted that sounded nice to her—Teedie Lete, Phebea Peadeo, Speackekey Leprlyo, and Aterryryee Roseendy were among her flock. She wrote poems for them and poems about them. And she kept them safe in a cellar she dug beneath her simple house, accessed through a trap door in her floor.

She lived on the small income she made from selling the eggs they laid. Then she repaid them, when the time came, by burying each bird with full honors in a wooden casket, in a grave she marked with a carved headstone. Nancy didn't want her "friends" to pass unremembered, so she collected their stories (and her own) in small books she carefully illustrated in her distinctive style. The island economy struggled then foundered following the Civil War, but Nancy worked on.

She was odd but indomitable. Toward the end of her life (she died in 1890) she began selling her self-published books to the increasing number of summer people visiting the island. Her homey eccentricity charmed the tourists and her struggles touched them. Almost a century later, Walter Magnes Teller penned a biography of Nancy based on her writings. In *Consider Poor I,* the biography, Nancy is quoted poetically offering the following dietary advice:

> You needn't talk against milk, if you
> make your victuals of water, what you
> put with water won't go half so far, and
> awful eating and distress ailing folks,
> and no nourishment to it. Make your
> victuals of milk, and what you put with
> milk will go twice as far, and good
> eating and nourishment to it. Milk is
> cooling to health, and strengthening,
> other victuals distress my stomach,
> because I am out of health; milk agrees
> with me, other victuals distress me. I
> cannot eat bread, &c., I must have milk
> to live on or go without eating till I die.

Rhubarb Cocktail

Serves 4

Tart rhubarb is one of my favorite spring tastes. The pink stalks make a syrup that I like to use in cocktails and to flavor Yogurt Granita (page 36).

FOR THE RHUBARB SYRUP
¾ cup sugar

2 pounds rhubarb, trimmed and chopped

FOR THE COCKTAILS
Ice cubes

8 ounces (½ cup) vodka

About 32 ounces (4 cups) seltzer

Lemon peel, pith removed, cut in strips

Make the rhubarb syrup. Combine the sugar and 2 cups water in a large pot and bring to a boil over high heat. Add the rhubarb and stir to make sure the sugar dissolves. Cover the pot, lower the heat just a little, and boil until the rhubarb softens, about 5 minutes. Pull the pan off the heat and allow the rhubarb to cool in the covered pot. Mash the rhubarb, then strain the juice through a double layer of cheesecloth into a small saucepan. Bring the juice to a boil over medium-high heat, then reduce until the juice is concentrated and syrupy and you are left with about 2 cups. Taste the syrup and adjust the sugar if necessary. Cool the syrup in the pan. Transfer to a container and refrigerate until well chilled.

Make the cocktails. Pour a generous tablespoon chilled rhubarb syrup into each of 4 chilled glasses. Add ice, vodka, and seltzer to taste. (It's a good drink even without the vodka!) Stir, then serve with a lemon strip in each glass. Refrigerate or freeze the remaining rhubarb syrup.

Potted Duck with Radishes

Serves 4 to 8

Jefferson Munroe raises a variety of birds on the Good Farm in Tisbury. I get my ducks as well as most of my chickens from him. In this recipe, duck legs are slow-roasted and wind up like a confit. The tender meat would of course be very good on toasted bread, but in April I yearn for vegetables, so I serve it with thinly sliced radishes.

> 2 tablespoons neutral oil, such as canola
>
> 1 medium onion, sliced
>
> 1 shallot, sliced
>
> 6 cloves garlic, peeled
>
> 4 bay leaves
>
> 10 sprigs fresh thyme
>
> 2 duck legs
>
> Kosher salt
>
> Freshly ground black pepper
>
> 4 radishes, thinly sliced

Heat the oven to 350°F. Warm the oil in an ovenproof pot with a lid over medium heat. Add the onion, shallot, and garlic cloves. Cook, stirring occasionally, until the onion begins to soften, about 4 minutes. Add the bay leaves and thyme. Season the duck legs liberally with salt and pepper and arrange them, skin-side up, over the onion mixture. Cover the pot and put it in the oven. Roast until the meat begins to pull from the bone, about 1 hour. Uncover and cook until the duck and onions are nicely browned, about 15 minutes more.

Remove the pot from the oven. Let it rest, covered, for 10 minutes. Take the legs from the pot and pick the meat from the bones (I like to chop the skin and mix that with the meat). Pull out and discard the thyme sprigs and bay leaves. Return the meat to the pot and mix it with the onion and rendered fat. Season with salt and pepper and serve warm or at room temperature with the sliced radishes.

Pea Green and Pancetta Salad

Serves 4

It is the crisped pancetta in the warm dressing that makes this salad so good—
that and the first, tender, fresh pea greens you can get your hands on.

> 3 tablespoons extra-virgin olive oil
>
> 1 ounce pancetta, diced
>
> 1 teaspoon minced lemon zest
>
> Freshly ground black pepper
>
> About 2 tablespoons fresh lemon juice
>
> About 5 ounces pea greens (about ¾ cup)
>
> Kosher salt

Heat a skillet over medium-high heat. Add 2 tablespoons of the olive oil
and the pancetta. Reduce the heat to medium and cook until the pancetta is
crisp, about 2 minutes. Remove the pan from the heat and add the
remaining 1 tablespoon oil along with the lemon zest. Season the dressing
with black pepper and lemon juice to taste.

Place the pea greens in a serving bowl and season with salt. Add the
dressing, toss, and serve.

Roast Chicken with Mushrooms and Baby Arugula

Serves 4

The chickens I get from the Good Farm — Cornish rock cross hens — are so flavorful you don't have to do anything more than salt them and roast them. But when I have the time I prefer to do the salting the night before, both on and under the skin. I find this makes the roasted bird extra crispy.

1 chicken, 3½ pounds

4 ounces shiitakes (or other firm mushrooms), stems removed and reserved

Kosher salt

Freshly ground black pepper

About 5 tablespoons extra-virgin olive oil

About 8 cups loosely packed trimmed arugula

Juice of 1 lemon

A day before you plan to serve the chicken, separate the skin from the meat by gently running your fingers between the two. Slice 2 of the shiitake to roast with the chicken later. Mix about 1 teaspoon salt and 1 teaspoon pepper together. Using your fingers, rub the salt mixture into the chicken, underneath the skin. Distribute the thinly sliced shiitakes under the skin over each breast. Put the chicken on a plate and season all over and inside the cavity with salt and pepper. Refrigerate, uncovered, overnight.

Remove the chicken from the refrigerator an hour before cooking to allow it to come up to temperature a bit. Heat the oven to 450°F.

Chop the reserved mushroom stems and put them in the chicken's cavity. Heat a skim of oil, about 2 tablespoons, over high heat in an ovenproof skillet big enough to hold the chicken pretty snugly. Put the chicken in the pan, breast-side up. Cook for 30 seconds, then take the chicken off the heat and baste it with the hot pan juices. Put the chicken in the oven and roast, basting every 10 minutes, for 30 minutes.

Thickly slice the remaining mushrooms and add them to the roasting pan. Roast together until the chicken juices run clear when the thigh is pricked, about 15 minutes longer, then let the chicken rest in the pan for 15 minutes.

Put the arugula in a bowl, season lightly with salt, and dress with lemon juice and 2 to 3 tablespoons olive oil (it is also nice to add a tablespoon of the pan juices to the salad). Toss thoroughly. Carve the chicken and serve with the roasted mushrooms on top of the arugula salad.

Rhubarb Tarts

Makes 4 (4-inch) tarts

The key to rhubarb compote is first macerating the fruit with sugar, then cooking the juice until it is almost a caramel. Only then do you add the rhubarb—this way it never overcooks.

FOR THE RHUBARB COMPOTE
1 pound rhubarb stalks, trimmed
½ cup sugar

FOR THE TART SHELLS
Flaky Pastry Dough (page 92)
1 egg, beaten
About 1 tablespoon turbinado sugar for finishing

FOR THE FILLING
½ cup fromage blanc (or cream cheese), warmed to room
    temperature
1 egg yolk
1 teaspoon honey

Macerate the rhubarb for the compote. Cut the rhubarb on the bias into pieces about 1½ inches long. Put the rhubarb in a bowl, add the sugar, and toss together. Set aside in a warm place to macerate, at least 1 hour.

Heat the oven to 400°F.

Prepare the tart shells. Divide the pastry into 4 pieces. Roll each portion out on a floured work surface into a rectangle about 4 by 5 inches. Score the center of each rectangle, leaving a perimeter rim about 1 inch wide on all sides. Put the tart shells on a baking sheet and chill for at least 30 minutes.

Make the filling. Mix the cheese, yolk, and honey together in a bowl.

Assemble the tarts. Spoon cheese filling onto the center of each shell, dividing it evenly and spreading it, stopping just short of the edges. Brush the perimeter rim of the tarts with the beaten egg then sprinkle with the turbinado sugar. Bake until the crusts are golden, about 30 minutes.

Finish the compote. Strain the rhubarb juice into a pan. Reserve the fruit separately. Bring the juice to a simmer over medium-high heat and allow it to reduce until it caramelizes and thickens into a syrup, about 5 minutes. Add the rhubarb to the pan, stir to coat with the syrup, and cook just until the rhubarb is tender. Start checking after 2 minutes. Pull the pot off the heat and allow the compote to cool slightly then spoon it onto each tart and serve.

LONGER DAYS

May

slivered peas
spinach & new potatoes

shiitake soup
parsley & soft-cooked egg

pork shoulder

fresh ricotta blintzes
&
cherries

SUNDAY JOBS

After I quit the city and moved back to Beetlebung to learn to farm, Sunday became the day Poppy and I went to the dump. It's a short drive up Middle Road and we would go right when it opened at 1:00 p.m. One o'clock worked for Poppy because it gave him time to get home from church and change his hat. He famously wore a long-brimmed sword-fisherman's cap to keep the sun off his bald scalp. For church he wore his "new" hat: red and proud; not to be confused with his everyday hat, the same, though long ago faded to pink and stained with grease and grass. In fact, Poppy and Gaga stopped attending Sunday services toward the end of his life, but he'd always remark on how convenient the schedule was as we drove over.

When we'd get to the dump I'd unload the truck and Poppy would start to scan the piles of discard for items of possible value. As soon as I'd cleared out the back Poppy would start piling things in: discarded wire for trellises, old hoses to be mended then used, pieces of wood, old tools, metal scrap, and different odds and ends he had no plan for but thought he might eventually use. Before we knew it we'd have more in his truck than we'd arrived with.

All the best farmers I know share Poppy's aversion to waste and a corresponding delight in efficient, ingenious solutions. Part of it is an economic necessity of small farming, but it goes beyond that. Rebecca Miller and Matthew Dix are a perfect example. Rebecca and Matthew run North Tabor Farm. They are raising their three terrific kids while Rebecca completes a master's degree and Matthew works days as conservation foreman for the Martha's Vineyard Land Bank. The rest of their time they tend their farm—famous for its meticulously grown greens.

A few years back, Matthew became unhappy about how much water they were using to wash the salad mix, a mainstay of their farm's economy. He began to wonder whether there wasn't something he could do with it all. He thought about it, then did some research, and decided that mushrooms might be the answer to his waste problem. He mailed away for spores and started them on oaks (downed trees he gathered from around his property or as he cleared trails on the conservation lands). He soaked the wood with wash water then seeded the spores. It was a nice, smart solution. North Tabor now produces the best shiitakes I have ever eaten, while "recycling" the way people have here for a very long time.

Spring Pea, Spinach, and Potato Salad

Serves 4

You can use snow peas or snap peas for this salad, which I like to make throughout the spring. I sliver raw peas, pods and all, on the bias, and mix them into the salad for a little crunch. (If your peas are mature, remove the fibrous "string" that runs the length of each pod before cutting them.)

> 12 new potatoes, scrubbed
>
> Kosher salt
>
> 4 ounces snow peas or snap peas, cut on the bias
>
> About 4 tablespoons red wine vinegar
>
> 2 tablespoons finely chopped onion
>
> About 4 tablespoons extra-virgin olive oil
>
> 4 cups loosely packed baby spinach
>
> Freshly ground black pepper

Put the potatoes in a pot, add water to cover, and season with salt. Bring to a boil over high heat, reduce the heat, and simmer until the potatoes are tender, 10 to 15 minutes.

While the potatoes are cooking, put 1 tablespoon of the vinegar in a small bowl. Add a pinch of salt.

Put the onion in the small bowl of vinegar and let marinate for 5 minutes. Add the peas and 1½ tablespoons of the olive oil to the onions. Mix and reserve.

Put the remaining 3 tablespoons of vinegar in a large bowl. Add a pinch of salt.

Drain the potatoes and transfer to the large bowl with the vinegar, along with 2 tablespoons of the olive oil; toss gently but thoroughly. Lift the potatoes out of the bowl (leaving the dressing behind) and arrange on 4 plates. Add the spinach to the dressing remaining in the large bowl. Season the spinach with salt and toss to coat (taste a leaf; if it is too dry, add a little oil and a splash more vinegar — but keep in mind the marinated peas will be served on the spinach).

Using the back of a spoon or your hand, smash the potatoes on the plates. Season them with a little salt and pepper. Arrange the spinach on the potatoes, then finish each salad with the marinated onions and peas and serve.

Mushroom Soup with Parsley and Egg

Serves 4

North Tabor Farm's shiitake mushrooms inspired this recipe. Replace the chicken stock with water for a vegetarian version — but if you do, increase the quantity of mushrooms to make sure you get a nice round flavor. Vegetarian or not, you can make the stock ahead when you have mushroom stems on hand, then freeze it.

> 6 shiitake mushrooms
>
> 2 white mushrooms, sliced (or you can use more shiitakes and stems)
>
> 6 cups homemade chicken stock (see page 140; this is not a soup I'd make with canned broth)
>
> 4 eggs
>
> 1 cup loosely packed fresh parsley leaves
>
> About 4½ tablespoons extra-virgin olive oil
>
> 1 medium onion, diced
>
> 2 small carrots, scrubbed, trimmed, and diced
>
> 2 small celery stalks, leaves reserved, stalks diced
>
> Kosher salt
>
> Freshly ground black pepper
>
> ½ teaspoon minced garlic
>
> 4 slices toasted country bread

Separate the shiitake caps and stems. Reserve the caps. Trim the stems, then chop and transfer to a large saucepan. Add the sliced white mushrooms and stock and bring to a boil over high heat. Lower the flame and simmer until the stock is flavorful, smells woodsy, and has reduced by a cup, about 10 minutes. Turn the heat off; cover the pot and let the stock steep for 20 minutes. Strain and reserve.

Soft cook the eggs. Bring a small pot of water to a boil. Add the eggs and simmer for 6 minutes. Drain the eggs, rinse under cold water, and peel. Put the eggs in the refrigerator to let the yolks set, about 20 minutes.

Refill the pot with water and bring to a boil over high heat. Add the parsley and blanch until the water returns to a boil. Drain and rinse in cold water. Chop the parsley and reserve.

Heat a skim of olive oil in the large saucepan over medium heat. Add the onion, carrots, and celery and sweat (cook gently until soft), about 15 minutes. Season with salt and pepper. Add the mushroom stock and bring to a simmer. Reduce the heat to low, cover, and simmer for 10 minutes.

Dice the mushroom caps. Heat a skim of oil in a skillet over medium-high heat. Add the diced mushrooms and season with salt. Cook the mushrooms until they are tender and beginning to crisp, about 2 minutes. Remove the pan from the heat, add the minced garlic, and mix well. Add the parsley and enough olive oil to moisten the mushroom mixture, about 2 tablespoons. Adjust the seasoning with salt if necessary.

Break or cut the eggs in half. Put half an egg in each of 4 bowls. Ladle soup over the eggs. Spoon the mushroom mixture onto the slices of toasted bread and put them on the eggs in the bowls. Top each with a second half egg, sprinkle with a few grains of salt, and serve.

Roasted Pork Shoulder

Serves 4 to 6

It's the fat in this delicious cut of meat that will keep things moist, allowing you to cook it slowly and develop the flavor. Look for a skin-on shoulder and it will be even more unctuous. The bones, which will almost fall off when the meat is done, add additional flavor—as always, they belong to the cook to snack on as the meat rests or after dinner as you wash up. Save any leftovers from the shoulder for Pulled Pork on Biscuits (page 273).

    1 bone-in, preferably skin-on, pork shoulder, 4 to 5 pounds
    Kosher salt

Heat the oven to 300°F. Score the skin of the pork, making crosshatch incisions through the skin and fat but stopping short of the meat. Do the same on the fat cap if you have a skinless cut. Season the meat all over with salt. Stand the shoulder skin-side up in a large roasting pan. Roast for 2 hours. Lay the shoulder on its side (cut-side down) and add ½ cup of water to the pan. Continue roasting for another hour. Flip the shoulder over and roast, basting occasionally, for 1 hour longer. Stand the meat back up so it rests on the bones with the skin up. Roast for about 1 hour longer, until the pork is tender and begins to pull away from the bone, tenting the meat and skin with foil if they start getting too dark. Allow the pork to rest for 30 minutes. Then slice off (or pull) the meat and serve.

Cheese Blintzes

Makes 8 or more blintzes

Looking through *The Foxfire Book of Appalachian Cookery* (Linda Garland Page and Eliot Wigginton), published in 1984, got me thinking about making cheese to fill blintzes. *Foxfire* is a great old book, part of a series that grew out of a high school folk-history project started in the mid-sixties in Georgia. The idea was that students would talk to older family members, neighbors, and acquaintances and learn about traditional ways of doing things, then write up the information. The Appalachian tales, crafts, and recipes the students recorded are different from what I know here in New England, but I find the reverence for tradition appealingly familiar.

FOR THE BATTER

1 cup all-purpose flour

1 tablespoon whole wheat flour

3 tablespoons sugar

3 eggs, beaten

3 cups milk

FOR THE RICOTTA

3 cups whole milk

1 cup heavy cream

1 teaspoon sea salt

3 tablespoons freshly squeezed lemon juice

FOR THE FILLING AND TOPPING

About 2 tablespoons honey

3 cups fresh cherries, halved and pitted

1 to 2 tablespoons sugar

1 tablespoon brandy (optional)

Butter for cooking the blintzes

Prepare the batter. Combine the all-purpose and whole wheat flours in a large bowl. Whisk in the sugar and eggs, then gradually whisk in the milk. Cover the bowl and put somewhere warm to rest the batter for at least 1 hour.

Make the ricotta. Combine the milk, cream, and salt in a small saucepan and heat over medium heat to 190°F (check it with a candy thermometer). Remove the pan from the heat and add the lemon juice. Stir just to combine, then let the mixture stand until the milk curdles, at least 5 minutes. Spoon the mixture into a double layer of cheesecloth. Hang the bag over a bowl to catch drips and set aside until the cheese is nicely firm, about 1 hour. (Discard the liquid.) Refrigerate the ricotta in a covered container until ready to use.

Make the filling and topping. Mix 1 tablespoon of the honey into the ricotta (more honey if you want it sweeter) and set aside at room temperature. Combine the cherries and sugar (the exact amount will depend on how sweet the cherries are) and add the brandy, if using; mix gently and set aside to macerate for at least 10 minutes.

Make the pancakes and assemble the blintzes. Heat a tablespoon of butter in a medium, slope-sided skillet (a crepe pan works perfectly). When the butter is frothy, spoon enough batter into the pan to coat the surface (about 2 tablespoons), swirling to spread the batter evenly. Cook until the first side begins to brown, about 4 minutes. Flip and cook until the second side begins to color, about 2 minutes more. Transfer the pancake to a plate and top with a tablespoon or so of the cheese filling. Fold in the sides and then roll the pancake around the filling to form a blintz. Keep the filled blintz warm at the back of the stove or in a very low oven. Repeat cooking and forming the rest of the blintzes with the remaining batter and additional butter as needed.

Serve the blintzes warm, topped with the macerated cherry topping. (Alternatively, the blintzes can be filled in advance then heated in a 350°F oven for 20 minutes before serving.)

menu

first

BABY LEEK, ASPARAGUS, AND PEA GREEN
SOUP

second

PICKLED CARROTS & GRIBICHE ON
ASPARAGUS TOAST

third

ROASTED
LEMON & FLUKE

fourth

WATERCRESS
PANZANELLA

to finish

CREAM & CHERVIL ON
STRAWBERRIES & SHORTCAKE

JUNE 15

WATERCRESS

My favorite spot to pick watercress is in Menemsha. That's all I'm going to say in the way of directions, except to suggest you follow the deer paths — look for snapped branches and other signs of fresh passage. These eventually lead to more commonly used avenues, where the tracks have beaten a trail and the leaves have been trampled flat, and then ultimately on to what I'll call a deer highway, where the bark is stripped from the trees and the ruts are defined by bare dirt so the way through the woods resembles a cleared footpath. This will lead you to the stream and to the spots where watercress grows — places you will be sure to find some before the weather gets too warm.

Peppery wild watercress is so much better than cultivated that I would harvest it regularly even if I didn't much like to, but that is not my problem. Clambering through the brambles before the leaves are out is pure pleasure. I am renewed in places other people seem not to care to go. I feel at home in the damp spots watercress grows — in the woods, near flowing, shallow water clean enough to drink on a hot day. So I will seize any excuse to trot through the trees to the streambed. This year I spotted the first green leaves in mid-April, before the last snow, about three weeks after the spring peepers began their choir practice, just when the skunk cabbage started to look like actual cabbage (which it is not, so don't ever eat it). I picked watercress all through the spring, getting the last of it later than usual, after Memorial Day, when the heat finally came to stay in June.

Leek and Asparagus Soup

Serves 4

The weather in June can swing from summery to rainy and quite chilly. It's been chilly this year. This soup, made with gently cooked leeks, pea leaves, young asparagus, and a little potato, is the perfect thing to fight the damp. It is quietly tangy. I bring that out by finishing the soup with yogurt. If you like, add a soft sweet herb. I like chervil.

4 small new potatoes, scrubbed and halved

Kosher salt

3 tablespoons extra-virgin olive oil

2 small cloves garlic, sliced

3 medium leeks

1 pound very thin young asparagus spears, trimmed

2 cups loosely packed young pea leaves

1 teaspoon grated lemon zest

About 3 tablespoons yogurt

Freshly ground black pepper

About ½ teaspoon lemon juice

Put the potatoes in a saucepan with salted water to cover by about an inch and bring to a boil over high heat. Reduce to a simmer and cook until the potatoes are tender, about 12 minutes. Drain and reserve.

Heat 1 tablespoon of the olive oil in a saucepan over medium heat. Add the garlic and toast until it is fragrant and golden, about 3 minutes. Transfer to a small bowl and reserve.

Trim off the leek greens and roots. Slice the leek whites in half lengthwise and then slice. Wash the sliced leeks thoroughly in several changes of water. Heat the remaining 2 tablespoons olive oil in the saucepan over medium-high heat. Add the damp leeks and cook for a minute or two, then reduce the heat to medium and cook, stirring frequently, until they soften slightly, about 3 minutes. Add 6 cups of water, season with salt, and bring to a boil.

Reserve a quarter of the asparagus to finish the soup. Slice the rest and add to the pan. Allow the asparagus to simmer until they are bright green, about a minute, then add the pea leaves and ½ teaspoon of the lemon zest. Pull the pot off the heat and season the soup with salt and pepper. Puree the soup in batches using a blender or food processor. Taste and adjust the seasoning if necessary.

To finish the soup, thinly slice the reserved asparagus (the tips will crumble some; that's OK). Cut the potatoes into small pieces. Combine the asparagus and potatoes in a bowl. Add the toasted garlic, remaining ½ teaspoon lemon zest, and 2 tablespoons of the yogurt. Season with salt, pepper, and lemon juice and mix well. Meanwhile, warm the soup over low heat.

Divide the potato and asparagus mixture among 4 bowls. Ladle soup into each, reserving about 2 tablespoons in the pot. Mix that with the remaining 1 tablespoon yogurt, drizzle over the soup in each bowl, and serve.

Asparagus on Toast

Serves 4

Because my grandmother liked asparagus so much, my grandfather took special care with his plants. Now I am carrying on the tradition. For this recipe I like thin, young asparagus. I cook them in a skillet even when I am working over a grill to make sure the smoky flavor doesn't overwhelm, only heightens. I top the asparagus with *gribiche,* a French sauce, traditionally an emulsion of hard-boiled egg yolk and oil perked up with pickles and herbs. I like a rough-chopped version and prefer to use the whole egg. I quick-pickle my own carrots (which is very easy) and put them in the sauce, but if you prefer another pickle, don't hesitate.

FOR THE GRIBICHE

2 eggs

1 bunch fresh parsley, leaves picked and chopped

6 tablespoons extra-virgin olive oil

Kosher salt

3 scallions, finely chopped

Pickled Carrot (page 212), chopped; plus 1 tablespoon of the
    pickling liquid

FOR THE ASPARAGUS AND TOAST

16 thin asparagus spears, trimmed

2 tablespoons butter

½ lemon

Kosher salt

4 slices sandwich bread, toasted

Make the *gribiche.* Bring a pot of water to a rapid simmer over medium-high heat. Add the eggs and cook for 8 minutes. Drain, run under cold water, and peel. Refrigerate for at least 30 minutes to allow the yolks to set.

Mix together the parsley and olive oil in a medium bowl. Generously season with salt. Add the scallions, pickled carrot, and pickling liquid. Chop the eggs, stir into the *gribiche,* and season to taste with salt. (Makes about 1 cup.)

Keep the *gribiche* in the refrigerator until you are ready to serve. Use any leftover on crostini, sandwiches, or salads or as a sauce for poached fish.

Prepare the asparagus and toast. Cut the asparagus spears into 3-inch lengths. Heat a skillet over medium heat and add the butter. When it's melted, add the asparagus and cook, turning the spears in the butter until they are bright green and just tender but not yet soft, about 3 minutes. Season to taste with lemon and salt.

Place the asparagus on the pieces of toast, top with the *gribiche,* and serve.

Pickled Carrot

Makes 1 pickled carrot

Pickled carrots are a nice way to offset a rich ingredient like the eggs in the *gribiche* above. Keep a jar in your fridge and use them on crostini and in sandwiches.

> 1 medium carrot, scrubbed and cut in half lengthwise, then each
>   half cut into quarters or sixths)
> Kosher salt
> ½ cup apple cider vinegar
> 2 tablespoons gin
> ¼ teaspoon black peppercorns
> ½ teaspoon honey

Blanch the carrot in boiling salted water until almost tender, about 4 minutes. Drain, refresh in cold water, and transfer to a small bowl or jar.

Combine the vinegar, gin, and ½ cup water in a small pot and bring to a rolling boil over high heat. Add the peppercorns and honey. When the honey has dissolved, pour the pickling liquid over the carrots. Cover and set aside for at least 1 hour, then refrigerate. The pickle will keep for a month in the refrigerator.

Spring Panzanella

Serves 4

This bread salad is the thing to make at the end of watercress season, when it is warm enough to get the first cherry tomatoes. It's also a terrific way to repurpose stale bread. When I worked at Babbo, we made panzanella with crusts and ends, diced early in the day then set out to dry. Toasting fresh bread in the oven also works. This salad was originally born out of thrift, but it is not the place to be stingy with the oil and vinegar — I use plenty of both.

About 2½ cups cubed country bread

About 5 tablespoons extra-virgin olive oil

Freshly ground black pepper

1 small red onion, halved and thinly sliced

¼ cup red wine vinegar

Kosher salt

2 cups cherry tomatoes, halved

About 2 cups loosely packed trimmed watercress

Heat the oven to 375°F. Arrange the bread in a single layer on a baking sheet. Drizzle with 1 tablespoon of the olive oil and season with pepper. Toast in the oven until the bread is golden, about 25 minutes.

In a small bowl, combine the onion and vinegar and season generously with salt. Set aside for at least 5 minutes.

Put the tomatoes in a large mixing bowl, season with salt and pepper, and add the remaining 4 tablespoons olive oil. Add the onion and vinegar, then the toasted bread. Toss the salad and set aside for 10 minutes or so.

Shortly before you plan to serve, cut the watercress into manageable pieces. Add the watercress to the panzanella and toss. Adjust the seasoning if necessary with salt and pepper, finish with more oil if you like, then serve.

Roasted Fluke

Serves 4

This dramatic dish is also very simple to make. The only thing that can be tricky is telling when the fish is done. Don't be scared to test by poking with the point of a knife; go in near the spine where the fish is thickest. If your knife slides in without resistance, the fish is done. Don't worry too much that you might overcook it; cooking a fish whole with the skin on keeps the flesh moist — a little over is better than under.

    1 fluke, 2½ pounds, scaled and gutted
    1 lemon, sliced, plus wedges for serving
    About 3 tablespoons extra-virgin olive oil
    Kosher salt

Pull the fish out of the refrigerator and let it come up to room temperature for about 30 minutes. Heat the oven to 450°F.

Arrange the lemon slices on a baking sheet. Put a rack over the slices (you want the fish up off the pan surface while it cooks; you could use a metal cake rack or fabricate a rack by making several tin-foil supports). Rub the fluke all over with the olive oil and season well with salt. Put it on the rack and roast until the fish is flaky when poked with a knife, about 15 minutes. Let it rest in the pan for 5 minutes, then fillet the fish or serve it whole with the roasted lemon slices and fresh lemon wedges.

Strawberry Shortcake

Serves 4

This biscuit recipe is one to remember. The dough is the one I use in the Blueberry Cobbler (page 250), and almost the same (with a few tweaks) as the one I use for the savory biscuits with pulled pork (page 274). The recipe makes five biscuits—that's one extra for the cook. Here, and whenever you make biscuits, have your ingredients cold and work quickly.

FOR THE BISCUITS

1 cup all-purpose flour

1½ teaspoons baking powder

1 tablespoon sugar

Small pinch of salt

3 tablespoons cold butter, cut into cubes

½ cup heavy cream

1 egg, beaten

FOR THE STRAWBERRY COMPOTE AND TOPPING

1 pound strawberries, trimmed

About 1 tablespoon sugar

⅓ cup heavy cream, softly whipped

Chervil for serving (optional)

Prepare the biscuits. Heat the oven to 400°F.

Mix the flour, baking powder, sugar, and salt in a large bowl. Using a pastry blender or your fingers, work the butter into the flour mixture until it resembles peas. Add the cream and stir until the mixture comes together.

Turn the dough out onto a floured work surface and form into a ball. Roll the dough out until it is about 1 inch thick, fold it in half, and then roll again to 1 inch. Cut out rounds using a 2½-inch biscuit cutter or highball glass and arrange on a baking sheet. Brush the top of each biscuit with beaten egg. Bake until the biscuits rise, about 10 minutes, then rotate the pan and continue baking until the biscuits are flaky and golden, about 10 minutes more.

Prepare the strawberry compote. Reserve half of the berries — the most beautiful ones — to add, uncooked, to the shortcakes later. Roughly chop the remaining strawberries and put in a saucepan. Add the tablespoon of sugar (a little more if the berries are tart) and 1 tablespoon water. Cook over medium-high heat until the berries soften, about 7 minutes. Set the berry compote aside to cool.

Assemble the shortcakes. Quarter the reserved strawberries. Cut 4 biscuits in half. Fill each with a spoonful of compote and a layer of whipped cream, then top with the fresh strawberries and the second half of the biscuits. Serve garnished with fresh chervil if desired.

HIGH SUMMER

browned romanesco & pea pesto

rock crab & summer squash spaghetti

lamb chops & blackened eggplant

herb & cucumber farro salad

fresh mint ice cream

the fourth
of july
in the
beetlebung
greenhouse

RETURNING HOME

I had been growing food on a small plot in the corner of the farm for a couple of summers when my Aunt Marie told me she was ready to call it quits. She'd always lived in Vermont but drove down every summer to work on Beetlebung with Poppy. After thirty-five years she was tired. She saw my interest and thought it might be time to pass the torch. She asked me if I would step in, and I did.

I wasn't prepared and I knew it. Although I had always helped out and had been trying to get serious the last several years, I had a lot to learn about farming. I was hesitant, but I decided that this was the push I needed. So I dove in and started trying to figure out how to coax the best from our beautiful but slightly eccentric five-acre plot — something Poppy and Marie had spent their lives at.

I knew enough to know the fences needed to be strengthened (the deer population seems to increase annually) and the irrigation improved, so that winter I set to work on the essentials: reinforcing broken stakes and mending hose links. And I built a greenhouse — really a hoop house — from lumber I found on the beach, reused hoops from another farm, plastic sheeting salvaged from a large operation's waste pile, and old doors Poppy had stacked in the barn God knows how long ago.

In the spring we started seeds in the tempered climate, beginning with leafy greens. I worked hard and got help from friends. By Memorial Day we were in good shape with radishes, pea greens, baby kale, and lots of young tender chard.

The goal was straightforward: to have the food we produced reach people's kitchens in a state of utter freshness. We harvested lettuces at dawn and never sold anything at the stand more than 12 hours after it was picked. The stand was first-come, first-served. At the beginning we wrote the prices on a chalkboard, but after drizzles and downpours we took to using permanent marker on shingle scraps. We couldn't afford the time away from the crops or other work to wait on customers, so we left a cash box for making change and relied on the honor system; it worked.

I got up early but still cooked late in well-appointed homes across the island, making money as a private chef to pay for the farm. I cooked our vegetables along with fish and meat my friends caught and raised. I relied on the skills I'd acquired in my twenties working in restaurant kitchens in New York, California, and Europe. I had learned to meticulously manipulate ingredients into delicious

meals. My forearms were scarred in those years off-island, burned on oven doors and racks. In restaurants these scars represented a badge of shared experience and honor, reminders of the price of creativity. I felt pride and pressure as I worked in renowned kitchens, preparing intricate dinners for paying customers who themselves worked hard to afford them. But that summer things began to change. I started cooking what I grew, and the cooking became easy.

I found I could show up for a dinner party an hour before it was scheduled with a truck filled with beautiful ingredients and the meal seemed to cook itself. The food was so remarkable that each vegetable and every piece of fish seemed to declare what should be done with it, mostly arguing in favor of not very much. Meals began with crudo or crostini topped with whatever was perfectly ripe; then came salads — fresh, dressed simply, tossed, and served; fish followed — fluke or bluefish or bass caught that morning; or meat — pasture-raised lamb or beef or Berkshire pork, grilled or roasted and served with whatever was best in the garden. The preparations were not complicated. But because the ingredients were so fine the dishes were elegant.

On my nights off I would cook with friends at the farm. We were inclined to be a little playful and we fire-roasted venison (often road kill, sadly), or made pasta dough and rolled it with wine bottles, then boiled the noodles in a banged-up pot on a jerry-rigged grill. Or we feasted on raw fish, lots and lots of it. Chilmark, I realized that summer, had the perfect balance for me. I could be outside, know my meat, and meet those who caught the fish as it arrived on the docks. I could compose menus when I was done picking the last bush beans and still have time to cook everything perfectly. I realized it was a lot of fun feeding people who knew (or wanted to learn) how delicious fresh ingredients are. And it was gratifying to express — with each dish I served to friend, farmer, fisherman, or hunter — how special the food here is.

Halfway through the season, I had an idea. I decided to turn my night-off, farm cookouts into the "restaurant" I'd always wanted. The set-up was simple. We built a table — it needed to be wide enough to hold all the platters of food plus bouquets of Poppy's flowers, and long enough that everyone could sit together. My brother is a skilled carpenter and he helped me put legs on planks we found washed ashore.

We put the word out. That first night we spit-roasted a goat over wood we burned to embers. We served the meat with potatoes from Poppy's garden. We also served Great Pond oysters, greens harvested hours earlier, along with field tomatoes and grilled sea bass. We sat together, those of us who'd grown and cooked the food along with our friends and their friends, and we all picked the bones clean. We ate in the hoop house because threatening clouds hid the moon. Slightly dirty fingers and manicured nails alike were dressed in the glow of the lights hung from the roof, powered by extension chords, and transformed into "chandeliers" made of rusty colanders. Toward the end of our meal, when I thought everyone might want one last bite before moving to dessert, I grabbed a headlamp and walked outside and harvested an apron-full of baby carrots. We rinsed them quickly and ate them like candy.

It was at once so familiar, so special, and so nice. In some ways the evening was not so different from what my family had always done in the summer on the farm and in some ways it was like the impromptu farm dinners we'd been patching together. But in other ways it was different—it was more thought out and we were sharing what we loved beyond our circle. It was, I knew then, a place to begin.

Romanesco Cauliflower with Sweet Pea Pesto

Serves 4

Romanesco cauliflower takes a long time to grow and does best when the weather is not too hot. Most summers there is a happy moment when we can harvest both the first peas and baby Romanesco, and this is what I make.

About ⅓ cup neutral oil, such as canola

¼ cup roughly chopped green garlic (or spring onion or scallion tops)

½ teaspoon minced lemon zest

1 cup shelled freshly picked peas

Kosher salt

1 tablespoon lemon juice or more

6 heads baby Romanesco, trimmed and halved

6 spring onions or scallion whites, butterflied or halved lengthwise

High-quality fruity extra-virgin olive oil for serving

Make the pesto. Heat a coating of neutral oil, about 2 tablespoons, in a skillet over medium-high heat. Add the green garlic and sauté until softened, about 1 minute. Spoon the sautéed garlic into a food processor.

Add the lemon zest and half the peas to the hot oil in the skillet, toss to coat evenly, and season with salt. Add the peas to the processor along with 1 tablespoon lemon juice and pulse. Add the remaining peas and pulse again until the puree is smooth. Thin the pesto with a little water, about 2 tablespoons. Adjust the seasoning with salt and lemon juice and reserve.

Cook the Romanesco. Add more oil, about 2 tablespoons, to the skillet and heat over medium-high. Working in batches if necessary, brown the Romanesco, cut-sides down, moving the pan and adjusting the heat to maintain a moderate sizzle, until the first sides are golden, about 3 minutes. Season the Romanesco with salt, then turn each piece and continue browning until the vegetable is tender, about 10 minutes in all. Reserve the Romanesco on a plate.

Add a little more oil to the skillet if necessary. Add the spring onions, raise the heat to high, and cook until they are tender and browned on both sides, about 4 minutes. Remove the skillet from the heat and return the Romanesco to the pan. Toss once or twice in the pan off the heat to rewarm.

Arrange the Romanesco and spring onions on plates. Dress the vegetables with the pea pesto, drizzle with fruity olive oil, and serve.

Spaghetti with Crab and Zucchini

Serves 4 to 6

Vineyard waters are full of crabs, but few are sold on the island these days because lobsters fetch a better price. That leaves plenty of crabs around for those of us willing to catch and then pick our own. So that is what I advise you to do; or, use whatever type of crab is available locally.

½ pound picked crabmeat

1 jalapeño, seeded and minced

3 tablespoons extra-virgin olive oil

¼ cup loosely packed fresh mint leaves

2 medium summer squash (yellow squash or zucchini)

1 tablespoon red wine vinegar

¼ teaspoon minced garlic

Kosher salt

Freshly ground black pepper

12 ounces thick spaghetti or bucatini

⅓ cup loosely packed fresh basil leaves, cut in slivers

Juice of ½ lemon

Bring a large pot of water to a boil over high heat. Combine the crab and jalapeño in a small bowl. Add 1 tablespoon of the olive oil. Chop half the mint and add to the crab. Mix well and set aside.

Sliver the remaining mint and put in a second bowl. Trim the squash, then grate them using a large-holed grater, stopping short of the seedy core (reserve it for another purpose; see page 231). Add the squash to the bowl with the slivered mint. Add the remaining 2 tablespoons of olive oil, the vinegar, and garlic and season with salt and pepper.

When the water boils, add salt and the pasta. Cook until the pasta is al dente, about 7 minutes. Just before the pasta is done, heat a large skillet over medium-high heat. Add the marinated crab, the squash, and the slivered basil.

Drain the pasta, reserving some pasta water. Add the pasta and about 2 tablespoons cooking water to the crab mixture. Heat everything together, tossing to mix well. Season with salt, pepper, and lemon juice and serve.

USING THE CORE

I like to use the squash cores to make a simple vegetarian pasta. Heat a good amount of olive oil — ¼ cup — in a large skillet over medium heat while you heat your pasta water. Smash a garlic clove and add it to the oil. When the garlic is fragrant, add a pinch of crushed red pepper, 3 sprigs of oregano, and a sprig of rosemary. Chop the squash cores and add them to the oil, then season with salt and lots of pepper. Drop the pasta (spaghetti or penne is good) into the boiling water. While the pasta cooks, cook the squash, smashing it with the back of a spoon. Cook until tender and brown. When the pasta is al dente, drain it (reserving some of the cooking water). Add the pasta to the squash. Turn up the heat and add 2 tablespoons red wine vinegar and a little pasta water. Toss, adjust the seasoning, and serve with grated Parmigiano-Reggiano.

Grilled Lamb Chops with Burnt Eggplant Puree

. . . .

Serves 4

This eggplant puree is very versatile. I have used it to dress fresh summer tomatoes as a first course, as a starting point for crostini and sandwiches, and as an accompaniment to all kinds of grilled and roasted meats and fish.

1 small Italian eggplant, about 1 pound

1 small clove garlic, chopped

About 3 tablespoons neutral oil, such as canola

1 tablespoon extra-virgin olive oil, plus additional high-quality
    extra-virgin olive oil for finishing

About 2 teaspoons sherry vinegar

Kosher salt

Freshly ground black pepper

4 (1-inch-thick) lamb rib chops

Make the eggplant puree. Place the whole eggplant directly on an open flame— on a stove burner or grill (or in a pinch you could char the eggplant under a hot broiler). Cook until the first side is blackened, about 5 minutes. Turn the eggplant over about a quarter of the way and char the next side, about 5 minutes. Continue turning and charring the eggplant (the last two sides will go more quickly) until it is charred on all sides and the eggplant is soft. Carefully transfer the eggplant to a bowl to cool slightly. Remove and discard the stem.

For a dark intense puree, don't peel the eggplant; for a lighter colored, milder puree, peel away and discard some of the charred skin. Add the eggplant and garlic to a food processor or blender and pulse, adding 1 tablespoon of the neutral oil and the extra-virgin oil to smooth the mixture. Transfer the puree to a bowl and season with the vinegar, salt, and enough additional neutral oil to make the puree silky tasting. (The puree can be made several hours ahead. If you refrigerate it, bring it to room temperature before serving.)

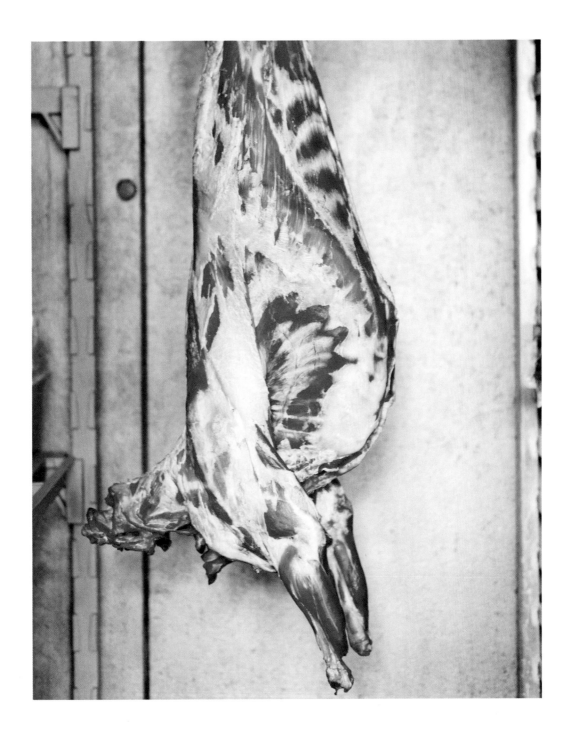

Grill the lamb chops. Build a hot fire in a grill. When the coals have burned to glowing embers, salt and pepper the lamb. Mop the grill with a little neutral oil, then stand the chops fat-side down on the grill. Render and brown the fat for about 1½ minutes. Place the chops meat-sides down and cook until the first sides are nicely browned, about 1½ minutes. Turn them over and cook the second sides, about 1 minute more. Test for doneness by touching the meat (it should give a little for medium-rare) or by making an incision and peeking. Continue cooking if necessary on a cool spot of the grill until the meat is how you like it. Transfer the chops to a plate; let rest for about 2 minutes. Serve the chops with the eggplant puree and a drizzle of extra-virgin olive oil.

Farro, Cucumber, and Herb Salad

Serves 4 generously

This is a really simple salad that is good early in the season when the first herbs pop up, but also perfect on those it's-too-hot-to-cook days of July. My one tip is to combine the ingredients one step at a time; this will create character in the salad and have a surprisingly important impact on the flavor.

2 cups farro

Kosher salt

4 scallions, white parts only, sliced

About 6½ tablespoons extra-virgin olive oil

2 large cucumbers, peeled and diced

2 tablespoons red wine vinegar

Minced zest of ¼ lemon

About 3 tablespoons lemon juice

1 cup loosely packed fresh basil leaves, roughly chopped

¼ cup fresh dill, roughly chopped

1 cup loosely packed fresh parsley leaves (left whole)

Freshly ground black pepper

Cook the farro as you would pasta, in lightly salted boiling water until it is tender, about 10 minutes. While the farro is cooking, combine the scallions and 1½ tablespoons of the olive oil in a large bowl. Drain the farro and add to the scallions. Mix well, season to taste with salt, then stir in half the cucumbers.

Put the remaining cucumbers in a small bowl and season with salt. Add the vinegar and 3 tablespoons of the olive oil. Mix to combine, then marinate for 20 minutes.

Add the lemon zest and lemon juice to taste to the farro. Add the remaining 2 tablespoons olive oil and mix well. Gently mix in the basil, dill, and parsley leaves. Add the marinated cucumber and toss well. Season with pepper and more salt and oil, if needed, and serve.

Mint Ice Cream

Makes about 1 quart

This ice cream is best when it's a little soft—right after it's been churned.

    1 cup whole milk

    3 cups loosely packed fresh mint leaves

    2 cups heavy cream

    ½ cup sugar

    4 egg yolks

Combine the milk and mint in a saucepan and bring to a simmer over medium heat. Remove the pan from the heat and set aside to steep for about 30 minutes. Strain the milk through a fine sieve, pressing the mint with the back of a spoon. Return the milk to the pan; discard the mint.

Add the heavy cream to the milk in the pan and warm over medium-low heat. In a separate bowl, whisk the sugar and egg yolks together until the mixture is pale yellow. When the milk mixture begins to simmer, temper the yolks by whisking in warm milk very gradually, a few spoons at a time at first, until you have added all the milk.

Pour the ice cream base back into the pan and bring to a simmer. Cook, stirring, until the ice cream base thickens. Test by dipping a wooden spoon into the base. Drag your finger over the spoon—if your finger has left a "track," it's thick enough. Pour the ice cream base into a metal bowl and cool over ice. Cover the bowl with plastic and refrigerate until the base is chilled thoroughly.

Process the ice cream in an ice cream maker according to the manufacturer's instructions, then serve.

High Summer 237

SUMMER MEAL

GARDEN **MINESTRONE**

·

GREEN BEANS & CHERRY **TOMATOES**

·

GRILLED PORK CHOPS & **LOBSTERS**

POTATO SALAD

·

BLUEBERRY COBBLER

COOKING OVER FIRE

The dinners we started hosting on the farm were outdoors or, when it rained, in our homemade greenhouse. We cooked over flame, but I didn't "grill" everything. I made pasta dough on a plank balanced between two drums—then cooked it, in a pot on the grates of whichever makeshift fire pit had space and was blasting hot. I roasted chicken on spits and stuck oysters in the coals. Everything had the special flavor that flame and smoke bring with them.

Cooking over an open fire isn't hard. It just takes some practice. Always start by building your fire four times bigger than you imagine you will ultimately want your pile of cooking embers. I like to use wood rather than charcoal when I can, and I use oak most often. Oak is easy for me to get because it grows all over Chilmark. Fruitwoods—cherry, apple, or pear—work well and add their own distinctive flavors; I use them at the end to finish things off. Keep away from wood with sap, like locust and pine. If wood isn't an option, go for charcoal—the smoke doesn't have the same complex flavor as wood smoke, but for me, any open fire is preferable to a stove.

Start building your fire in the center of your grill or cook pit; and don't worry if things look a little unruly. Leave enough space for oxygen to move around and help the fire spread. Cook where the wind boosts your operation just enough so there is no need for lighter fluid, but use it if you must. I work in layers, starting with wadded newspaper, then cardboard, then I add shingles (shingles work great and my brother is a carpenter so I have a good line on scraps), sometimes twigs, and finally small split kindling (small stuff—about an inch in width). I end with logs of all sizes, beginning with the smallest. Expect that these will need at least an hour and a half to burn down to embers (charcoal takes markedly less time). Be patient. Give your fire the time it needs, and add more logs if it burns down too much. Poke, prod, and reorganize as you go—this is the way to get the most even bed of coals. Once the flames subside, beat your embers up a bit. Hit them with whatever strong tool you have handy; I like a shovel. You want to break them up to expose all the surfaces to promote even burning because when you grill, you want a bed of coals, glowing right at the point that you question whether what you see is a flame or just a glow. If you are cooking meat, expect fat will melt and cause a flare-up or two, but an even bed of embers will keep this to a minimum.

Some advanced grillers rake their beds and organize descending levels of heat and flames; with a big grill you can do this, giving yourself plenty of room to navigate and find sweet spots. You don't have to rake, but you should pass your hand over the embers when they are just about ready and feel the variation in heat—find the cool spots in the corners and the incendiary areas in the middle.

Heat the grates in advance. This prevents sticking and ensures grill marks. Once your fire has burned down about half way, still flaming but not crazy, put the grill on top and burn off any debris remaining from your last adventure. Use a wire grill brush to remove the stubborn bits. Then, right before you start cooking, mop the grill with an oiled rag (use tongs and be prepared for flashes of fire).

Put your steak or chop, lobster or fish on the grill and set to it. Don't walk away. Watch what you are cooking and respond to what you see happening. Help things along, flipping and repositioning as you go. I like to snag a few choice bites as I "work," with a beer in my hand, the setting sun on my face, barefoot, my pants rolled up, and a sweater nearby in case the evening cools.

Summer Minestrone

Serves 4 generously

This soup is a garden in a bowl and substitutions should be made as the season progresses. It is nice hot, but it is also very good chilled. Served that way I like to wake it up with a splash of red wine vinegar just as it's served.

About 7 tablespoons extra-virgin olive oil

2 medium leeks, white parts only, quartered lengthwise and sliced

1 small yellow onion, diced

2 small cloves garlic, minced

Kosher salt

Freshly ground black pepper

2 medium carrots, scrubbed, halved lengthwise, and sliced

2 medium stalks celery, halved lengthwise and sliced

4 new potatoes, scrubbed, quartered, and sliced

¼ cup loosely packed parsley leaves

1 tablespoon marjoram leaves

1 medium zucchini, quartered lengthwise and sliced

¼ pound green beans, trimmed and cut into ½-inch lengths

1 cup spinach, chopped

2 tablespoons minced fresh mint

Red wine vinegar (optional)

Heat 3 tablespoons of the olive oil in a large pot over medium-low heat. Add the leeks and onions and cook, stirring occasionally, until they begin to soften, about 5 minutes. Add the garlic and some salt and pepper. Add the carrots and celery and another tablespoon or so olive oil. Cook, continuing to stir occasionally, until the carrots are no longer hard, about 5 minutes more. Add the potatoes and cook, mixing them with the other vegetables. Roughly chop the parsley and add 2 tablespoons along with the marjoram. Season again with salt and pepper, add the zucchini and green beans, and cook for about 5 minutes more. Add the spinach, mix well, and add water to cover, about 5 cups. Bring the soup to a simmer, adjust the heat, and allow it to cook until the vegetables are all tender and the flavors melded, about

10 minutes more. Adjust the seasoning with salt and pepper and keep warm or chill.

Make an herb pesto. Chop the remaining parsley more finely and combine it in a bowl with the mint. Season with salt and mix in 3 tablespoons olive oil. Serve the soup warm or chilled with the herb pesto, adding a little vinegar if you like.

Fresh Green Bean and Cherry Tomato Salad

Serves 4

An old farm trick: Hold a "farm fresh" bean up to your T-shirt. If it was picked that day it will stick like Velcro; if not it will fall to the ground. The drops should be washed and cooked, used for soups or stews, but the T-shirt-sticking beans are incredible raw; they are just what you want for this salad.

¾ pound cherry tomatoes, stemmed

Kosher salt

3 tablespoons red wine vinegar

6 tablespoons extra-virgin olive oil

½ pound green beans

1 cup loosely packed parsley leaves

Freshly ground black pepper

Cut the tomatoes in half and put them in a bowl. Season with salt and dress with the vinegar and then the olive oil. Mix gently and marinate for 5 minutes or so.

Snap off the tops and tails of the beans. Add the beans and parsley to the tomatoes. Season with pepper, toss gently, and serve.

Grilled Porterhouse Pork Chops

Serves 4

A porterhouse chop is a bone-in rib chop cut from the lower end of the loin through the backbone, so you get both tenderloin and loin. I like mine cut about 2 inches thick and find that two chops will feed four people — you'll just have to fight over the bones.

> Neutral oil, such as canola, for mopping the grill
>
> Kosher salt
>
> 2 (2-inch-thick) porterhouse pork chops, 2 to 2½ pounds

Build a fire in your grill and let it burn down to medium-high heat. Rub the grill with a little oil. Salt the chops and put them on the grill. Cook long enough to get grill marks, about 4 minutes, then rotate each chop a quarter turn. Cook the chops until they have nice crosshatched marks, about 4 minutes more. Flip the chops and sear on the second side, repeating the same process. Move them to a moderately hot part of the grill and cook until the second side is nicely browned, about 4 minutes more. Using tongs, balance the chops on their fatty edges. When the fat is nicely crisp and the meat is just cooked through, pull the chops off the heat and let them rest for 5 minutes.

Slice the pork, returning less cooked pieces along the bone back to the grill for a few minutes if necessary. Put the pork on a platter, pour any juices released while carving over the sliced meat, and serve.

Grilled Lobster

Serves 4

The tricky part about grilling lobster is getting the meat to cook evenly. I have learned to split the lobster (butterfly it, really), crack the claws, baste as I go, and always work over a moderate, never hot, fire. If I'm serving a mix of meat and fish, the lobsters go on last, after the coals have lost their fury, and I allot half a lobster per person — but you should suit yourself.

> 2 small lobsters, each 1¼ to 1½ pounds
>
> 3 tablespoons butter, plus more for serving
>
> Pinch cayenne pepper
>
> 1 lemon, cut in quarters
>
> Neutral oil, such as canola, for mopping the grill

Build a fire in the grill and let it burn down to medium heat. Lay a lobster on its back on a cutting board. Using a good sharp knife, cut through the belly down toward the tail. Go back to where you started and reverse directions to cut up through the top of the belly to (and through) the head. Try not to cut through the back shell. Using your fingers, spread and flatten the tail and body. Crack each claw in 4 places starting at the "hand" and moving down the "arm"; then wrap the claws with tin foil. Repeat, butterflying, and cracking, then wrapping the claws of the other lobster.

Put the butter, cayenne, and lemon in a small skillet. Set it in a cool corner of the grill to melt. Rub the grill with a little oil. Put the lobsters on the grill cut-sides down. Cook until the shells begin to become red at the edges, about 4 minutes. Flip the lobsters and cook, basting the tails with the melted butter, until the tails begin to curl, about 4 minutes more. Turn the lobsters back onto their cut sides and grill until the tail is cooked through, about 3 minutes more. Move the lobsters so the claws are centered over the fire and the tails are away from the heat and finish cooking the claws, turning the lobsters once or twice more and basting the tails with butter, about 6 minutes. Pull the lobsters off the heat and serve with additional melted butter if desired.

Potato Salad

Serves 4

This potato salad is best made ahead, so it is the side dish to make when you need to focus on your grilling. I like to use brown mustard seeds. They are nutty tasting and a bit spicier than yellow mustard seeds.

8 medium red bliss (or new) potatoes, scrubbed and halved or
    quartered
Kosher salt
¼ cup roughly chopped fresh dill
About ⅓ cup extra-virgin olive oil
About 1½ tablespoons apple cider vinegar
About 1½ tablespoons white vinegar
2 teaspoons brown mustard seeds, toasted over low heat

Put the potatoes in a pot and cover with water. Add salt, bring to a boil, and simmer over medium heat until the potatoes are tender, about 20 minutes. Drain the potatoes. When cool enough to handle, cut into bite-sized pieces.

Put the potatoes in a bowl and add the dill. Dress the salad with olive oil, cider vinegar, and white vinegar to taste. Add the mustard seeds and season with salt. Toss gently, checking the seasoning and adjusting as necessary. Serve at room temperature.

Blueberry Cobbler

Serves 4 to 6

This is a recipe that can be adapted according to the season. Virtually any berry will work, as will juicy stone fruits like plums, nectarines, and peaches. I make the cobbler in a small baking dish with 4-inch sides, but an 8-inch cast-iron skillet would also work.

FOR THE BISCUIT DOUGH
1 cup all-purpose flour

1½ teaspoons baking powder

1 tablespoon sugar

Pinch of salt

3 tablespoons cold butter, cut into cubes

½ cup heavy cream

1 egg, beaten

FOR THE FILLING
4 cups blueberries

⅓ cup sugar

¼ teaspoon minced lemon zest

Juice of ½ lemon

Heat the oven to 400°F.

Prepare the dough. Mix the flour, baking powder, sugar, and salt in a large bowl. Using a pastry blender or your fingers, work the butter into the flour mixture until it resembles peas. Add the cream and stir until the mixture comes together. Turn the dough out onto a floured work surface and form into a ball. Roll the dough out until it is about 1 inch thick. Fold it in half and then roll again to ½ inch. Cut the dough into rounds using a 2½-inch biscuit cutter or highball glass and arrange on a baking sheet.

Make the filling. Combine the blueberries and sugar in a small baking dish or skillet. Add the lemon zest and juice and mix well.

Arrange the dough rounds on top of the blueberries and brush with the beaten egg. Bake until the biscuits begin to color, about 15 minutes. Reduce the heat to 325°F and continue baking until the biscuits are golden and the berry mixture is bubbling, about 30 minutes. Serve warm or at room temperature.

SUNDAY

FISH CHOWDER

CHILMARK RIB-EYE

WHITE BEAN and SCALLION SALAD

WILTED and RAW BOK CHOY

summer berry and sweet bread pudding

GRILLED GRASS-FED STEAK

For the past several years, almost all the beef I've been cooking has been pasture-raised. I've learned through trial (and the occasional error) that pastured, grass-fed meat is different in important ways from the grain-fed beef I learned to cook in my twenties. You can see the difference. Look at a steak from a grass-fed cow and you'll see immediately that it is a very rich, dark red — almost like game. That vibrant color promises a healthfulness consistent with the more active life the animal lived. Pasture-raised beef is packed with omega-3 fatty acids, a beneficial form of cholesterol.

Along with the deeper color, you'll notice that grass-fed beef is leaner. A steak will be less tendered by fat, the meat a bit chewier, the gristle gristlier. While grain-fed animals live on a regimen aimed at fattening them up, field-fed cattle fend for themselves and wind up slimmer and more muscular. They are also subject to greater variation. If it's a hot, dry summer, the fat on a pastured cow will be nicely nutty, but there won't be much of it.

A steak cut from grazed animals tastes the way I think steaks are meant to. It tastes of the place it was raised, that year's weather, and, at its best, of the salt air coming off the Atlantic. My cousin Josh, Marie's son, raises his cows on leased grass and wildflowers mostly on Middle Road, not far from my house. His growing herd is my preferred source.

I love the flavor of Chilmark meat, but I've learned that less lubricating fat can mean it's easier to miss your mark when you cook it. And when it's cooked a little too long, it can wind up dry — in other words, grass-fed beef is less forgiving. So I've made some adjustments. I now am careful to err on the undercooked side. I'm not afraid to take my meat off the heat, let it rest, cut a piece, then put it back if I have to — no harm done. My other secret: Divide and conquer. I cut a rib eye in pieces, then cook each in the way that suits it best.

I begin by "temping" the steak — I pull it out of the refrigerator, and let it come up to room temperature for at least an hour. While the meat loses its chill, I build a fire. You can skillet-roast a steak, but it is hard to argue with the special magic fire brings with it. So I recommend that you set a blaze in your grill, fireplace, or even in a wheelbarrow.

Then I break down the rib eye. I start by cutting the bone from the meat. I do this in an intentionally rough way, leaving some substantial scraps attached. I season the scrappy bone with salt and pepper and put it on the grill, cooking it over moderate heat until the meat is slightly charred and beginning to pull away from the browned bone, about 10 minutes. The bone is a special bonus I save for myself, as I love gnawing on carcasses and gristly bits.

Once I've removed the bone, I use my knife to separate the outer and shoulder muscles that surround the round loin at the top of the steak. I'll call these my "cap" steaks. These portions of a rib eye connect the loin to the cow's shoulders and because these muscles get more exercise than the central loin they cradle, they are a little tougher and need to be cooked a little more gently, over more moderate heat. (The higher fat content and more regular marbling in grain-fed meat makes the variation between the loin and cap less pronounced.)

Next I trim away the thickest pieces of connective tissue from the steaks, I trim the tendon and most of the fat—anything white, not red. All this goes into a small skillet and then onto a cool corner of the grill to be rendered. I like to supplement my trimmings with grass-fed beef suet, a couple of extra ounces. I add a clove of garlic and a sprig of rosemary once the fat is melted. When the garlic is soft, I take the pan off the heat, add a pinch of salt, then cover it to keep it warm.

I salt and pepper the cap steaks and put them on a moderately hot part of the grill (a section where you can hold your hand 4 inches above the grill for no more than 5 seconds). Cook these steaks, turning them when they are nicely browned, about 5 minutes. Continue cooking the steaks, moving them to a cooler section of the grill if they are cooking too quickly, until they are just past medium-rare, still pink and juicy inside, 5 to 8 minutes more. Set the cap steaks in the warm rendered fat and let them rest there.

Rather than cook the loin of the rib eye in one piece, I separate it into its several lobes, tracing the seams of connective tissues with my knife. The number is a function of how far from the rump the steak was cut. Season the loin steaks with salt and pepper. Give your coals one last rake to create a hot spot, make sure whatever else you are planning to serve is ready to go, then grill the steaks quickly, turning them with tongs or your fingers—this way you can flip and test for doneness simultaneously. The loin is best rare, so expect it to take 3 minutes per side for a

2-inch-thick piece of meat. Once the meat comes off the heat, add the loin steaks to the skillet of seasoned fat and let them rest long enough to grab some flavor, about 2 minutes. Slice all the meat against the grain and serve while still warm.

Corn and Fish Chowder

Serves 4 generously

I add neither cream nor milk to this chowder, but because I start with a whole fish it is deeply flavored. If you can, divide the work over two days: make the stock first, then refrigerate it overnight and finish the soup the next day.

> 1 medium sea bass or other white-fleshed fish, about 1½ pounds,
>   scaled and cleaned
> 2 ears corn, husked
> 2 medium Yukon gold potatoes, scrubbed
> ½ bunch parsley
> 2 tablespoons butter
> 1 medium onion, diced
> Kosher salt
> 1 cup loosely packed basil leaves, roughly chopped
> Freshly ground black pepper

Make the stock. Put the fish in a big pot. Cut the corn from the cobs and reserve; put the cobs in the pot. Peel the potatoes, putting the peels in the pot. Reserve the potatoes in a bowl of water. Pick the leaves from the parsley; put the stems in the pot and reserve the leaves. Add water to cover the cobs, about 8 cups, and bring to a boil over high heat. Reduce the heat, and simmer until the fish is cooked through, about 15 minutes. Pull the stock off the heat and allow it to cool.

Strain the stock. Pick the fish from the carcass, discarding the skin and bones. Reserve the stock and fish in separate sealed containers in the refrigerator.

Finish the soup. Wipe out the pot, add the butter, and melt over medium-low heat. Add the onion and cook until slightly soft, about 5 minutes. Drain the potatoes, dice, and add to the pot. Season with salt and cook, stirring frequently, until the potatoes soften, about 12 minutes. Add the corn kernels and continue cooking until the corn is tender, about 5 minutes.

Begin adding the stock, just enough to cover the vegetables, about 4 cups. Allow it to come to a simmer over medium heat.

Add the fish to the soup, along with the remaining stock (add a little water if necessary to cover the fish and vegetables by an inch or so). Season with salt and pepper to taste and bring to a simmer. Roughly chop the reserved parsley leaves. Add half the parsley and basil to the pot. Divide the rest of the parsley and basil between 4 bowls. Ladle soup into each and serve.

Grilled Rib Eyes

Serves 4

I learned to cook a thick, marbled steak as a line cook working for Mario Batali at Babbo in New York City's Greenwich Village. We pulled Pat LaFrieda's beautiful grain-raised prime steaks out of the walk-ins to warm up a bit before service. We cooked them on a hot grill, let them rest, and carved them table-side — a home run every time. Since then I've started breaking down larger steaks in order to cook each segment perfectly. This is particularly essential when you are grilling lean pasture-raised beef.

> 2 bone-in grass-fed rib eye steaks, each about 2 inches thick, deboned and trimmed (bones and trim reserved), the "cap" steaks and loins separated as described on page 254
> 1 clove garlic, peeled
> 2 sprigs fresh rosemary
> Kosher salt
> Freshly ground black pepper
> Salsa Verde (page 260)

Allow the steaks to come to room temperature. Build a fire in the grill and let it burn down to moderate heat. Cook the bones until the meat is charred and beginning to pull away from the bone, about 10 minutes. Reserve to serve with the steak, or enjoy them while the meat is cooking.

Put the steak trimmings in a small skillet to render in a corner of the grill (add extra beef suet if you like). Add the garlic and rosemary once the fat is melted. When the garlic is soft, take the pan off the heat, add a pinch of salt and some pepper, then cover the pan to keep the rendered fat warm.

Salt and pepper the cap steaks and put them on a moderately hot part of the grill. Cook for about 5 minutes, then flip and cook until they are just past medium-rare, about 5 minutes longer, moving them to a cooler part of the grill to finish if they need a few extra minutes. Set the cap steaks in the rendered fat to rest.

Divide the loin of the rib eye into its several lobes (for more specific directions, see page 254). Season the loin steaks with salt and pepper. Cook the loin steaks on the hottest part of the grill for 3 minutes, then flip and cook about 3 minutes more for rare. Add the loin steaks to the skillet of seasoned fat and let them rest for 2 minutes. Slice all the meat against the grain and serve with salsa verde.

Salsa Verde

Makes about 1⅔ cups

Salsa verde is a fresh and pungent sauce that is perfect with grilled and roasted meat or fish. Feel free to use whatever mixture of herbs and greens looks best, and don't hesitate to add capers and anchovies if you want a more assertive sauce. Recently I have been finishing salsa verde with fresh, peppery radishes; for the details, see the variation below.

    2 small shallots, minced
    6 tablespoons red wine vinegar
    About ¾ cup chopped parsley (or a mixture of greens and herbs)
    About ¼ cup chopped mint (or arugula, or fennel fronds, or radish
        greens, or a mixture)
    Kosher salt
    About ¾ cup mild extra-virgin olive oil

Combine the shallots and vinegar in a bowl and set aside for about 10 minutes.

Combine the parsley and mint in another bowl. Season generously with salt, then mix in the shallots. Add enough oil to just cover and serve.

Variation: Radish Salsa Verde

Combine ½ cup minced shallots and ⅓ cup red wine vinegar in a bowl, season with salt, and set aside for 10 minutes. Mix in ¼ cup roughly chopped mint and ¼ cup roughly chopped parsley. Slice halved or quartered radishes (I like French radishes — but use what looks best), then mix them in. Add olive oil to just cover, adjust the seasoning with salt, then serve.

White Bean Salad

Serves 4

Somewhere along the line I got into the habit of "cooking" scallions and onions in a little vinegar before adding them raw to salads. I find that doing this not only tames their sharpness but also flavors the vinegar in a way that makes the salad more harmonious.

6 small cloves garlic, peeled

½ cup extra-virgin olive oil

Pinch crushed red pepper

2 bunches scallions, trimmed and halved lengthwise, then sliced

¼ cup white vinegar

Kosher salt

4 cups cooked white beans (see Cooking Beans, page 45)

Put the garlic cloves in a small pot. Add the olive oil and crushed pepper. Cook over low heat until the garlic is soft, about 12 minutes.

Combine the scallions and vinegar in a mixing bowl. Season with salt and set aside for about 10 minutes.

Add the beans (warm if you've just cooked a batch) to the scallions. Mix gently and let the flavors blend.

Spoon the oil and garlic over the beans. Mix gently, adjust the seasoning with salt if necessary, and serve.

Raw and Cooked Bok Choy with Anchovies

Serves 4

This is a great salad to make in the summer—it is at once both light and flavorful, but it is also a very good dish to remember in the colder months when bok choy is one of the few green vegetables you can find on market shelves that's good raw.

1 pound bok choy

1 lemon, ¼ teaspoon minced zest reserved

Kosher salt

3 anchovy fillets, finely chopped

About 2 tablespoons neutral oil, such as canola

Trim the bok choy and separate the leaves and stems. Roughly chop the leaves and reserve. Cut the stems into thin lengths on the bias and put them in a bowl. Cut the lemon in half and squeeze it over the bok choy stems. Season with a little salt and toss to mix.

Combine the lemon zest and chopped anchovies in a bowl. Season lightly with salt, add 1 tablespoon oil, and mix well.

Heat a large skillet over high heat. Add a skim of oil, the reserved leaves, and a little salt. Cook the leaves, tossing and stirring them, until they wilt, about 2 minutes. Season the leaves with about half of the anchovy mixture and lemon juice. Spoon the leaves onto plates.

Add the remaining anchovy mixture to the stems. Mound them on top of the leaves and serve.

TOMATOES

We see the first tomatoes here in late June. They are usually small Sungolds and they are often from Caitlin Jones's greenhouse. By early July my dad's buoy-trellised plants are ready to be picked. He grows the best tomatoes, favoring non-heirloom varieties that are big, red, and wonderful. Over the years I've tried to figure how he does it. I haven't got it down, but I do know some of his tricks. He spaces his plants far apart, and he babies them right from the start. He prunes them, defining one strong leader that usually looks spindly at first, but in the end produces massive amounts of fruit. I know he believes that growing the perfect tomato means giving the plant everything it needs. My dad treats his tomato plants with love and respect. He pampers them and is rewarded.

The best way to eat a good tomato is off the vine when it's still warm from the sun, with nothing on it. The second best way is on a piece of good toasted bread with Aioli (page 34), and a little sea salt. The third best way is to add another piece of bread and call it a sandwich.

As far as tomato salads go, I can get fancy but generally prefer not to. Instead, I like to find a creamy ball of burrata and put it on a plate with a roughly chopped perfect tomato, then wait a couple of minutes to let the juices mingle with the cheese. I finish things with plenty of sea salt and a great olive oil—pretty hard to beat.

By August tomatoes are everywhere, but I don't get sick of them. I eat the best ones simply, the slightly less than perfect chopped and tossed raw with beans or pasta and lots of herbs, and I always roast some. Then, finally, I take the end-of-the-season uglies (which you can usually get cheaply if you don't have plants of your own) and make sauce I know I am going to be happy to have in February.

Summer Pudding

Serves 6 to 8

This is an old-fashioned English dessert, both simple and refreshing. Mixed berries, whatever looks best, are layered with toasted bread then weighted to form a cake (an English "pudding"). I use Portuguese sweet bread, a grocery-store reminder of the Portuguese whaling men who settled here in numbers beginning in the 1800s. Brioche or challah would work equally well.

1 (1-pound) loaf sliced Portuguese sweet bread, crusts trimmed

8 cups summer berries, a mixture of raspberries, blueberries, blackberries, and roughly chopped strawberries

¾ cup sugar

Juice of 1 lemon

Toast the bread. Heat the oven to 350°F. Put the bread on baking sheets and toast in the oven until golden, about 20 minutes.

Cook the berries. Reserve 1 cup of berries and place the remaining in a saucepan with the sugar and lemon juice. Mix well and set aside for 10 minutes.

Place the pan over medium heat and cook the berries until they soften and their juices thicken slightly, about 15 minutes. Allow the cooked berries to cool.

Assemble the "pudding." Spoon a layer of cooked berries into a 2-quart high-sided casserole or flat-bottomed bowl. Arrange a layer of toasted bread on top of the berries, trimming the bread to fit. Put about a third of the reserved raw berries on the bread then repeat, layering cooked berries (and their syrup), bread, and fresh berries until you have enough for one last layer. In this final layer, top the cooked berries with the last of the fresh berries, then finish with toasted bread. Cover with plastic wrap, set the casserole or bowl on a plate (to catch wayward juices), and top with a small plate and a heavy weight. Chill the weighted pudding overnight.

Unmold the pudding. Run a knife around the sides, then invert a large plate over the casserole. Flip the casserole and plate, tap the bottom of the casserole and unmold the pudding onto the plate. Slice and serve.

PROGRAM

and

List of Premiums

offered by the

MARTHA'S VINEYARD
AGRICULTURAL SOCIETY

Menu

Fair Grounds - - - West Tisbury
August 18

- *FRIED SQUID* and *SWEET ONION*

- *PULLED PORK* on a *BISCUIT*

- *FISH TOSTADOS*

- *CORN* on the *COB*

- *BLACKBERRY PIE*

THEN AND NOW

The first agricultural fair on Martha's Vineyard was held in October 1858. It was a harvest festival, and more than 1,800 people (over half of the Vineyard's population) made their way to the middle of the island to congregate under tents. Herdsmen led cows, shepherds guided sheep, some folks rode horses, and many others came in carts or walked carrying chickens and flowers and vegetables and the bedrolls they used to camp out in the surrounding fields during the two-day event.

The draw was the opportunity for people to pit livestock, produce, and themselves against one another in what I imagine as a Farmers' Olympics, with tests of strength, skill, power, and pedigree. It was also a chance for a get-together—a great big party, before the inevitable hunkering down winter would bring. The gathering was such a success that they built a grange hall the very next year.

That's where the fair was held for most of Poppy's life (a new hall was raised to accommodate expanding crowds twenty years ago). Poppy loved the fair and never lost his childish delight in the annual celebration. He told us what it was like

when he was young, and about the foot races he won competing against other heavy-booted or bare-footed farmers' and fishermen's sons. But though he remembered it fondly, he didn't dwell on the past. Poppy served as president of the Ag Society in his middle years, then as a livestock judge (deciding the poultry face-offs was the hardest, he always said, as chicken farmers can get plenty heated). And all his life he enthusiastically entered his flowers and vegetables.

These days the fair is held over three days in late August. I have gone all my life, and every year it's packed with locals and summer people enjoying themselves from the time the first tickets go on sale until the last carnival rides shut down.

The food you eat when you go is in its own special category. It's a mix of enticing once-a-summer-delights, celebratory and seductive, and includes both island favorites and midway standbys. At the early fairs I'm guessing they ate roasted meat, grilled corn, and hand-churned ice cream; maybe oysters or chowder or slices of blackberry pie. Today you'll still find chowder, ice cream, and corn, but also burgers and tacos and fried this and that.

I confess I have a soft spot for fair food. It is tasty, especially so when made carefully with good local ingredients. So, I've reimagined my favorite guilty pleasures just a little. They would all still be a delicious treat to enjoy as you watch the ox-pull before you go on the Ferris wheel, but the recipes that follow go beyond their humble origins. Fish tostados, for example, are a great way to begin a serious meal if you make your own small tortillas (it is very easy). Crispy squid and onion slivers also make a nice starter, served with a small salad. Pork on biscuits is a great way to feed a crowd at supper. Blackberry pie is delicious any time. And so this "menu" is intended not as a meal, but rather as a starting place for creating summer repasts that share the fun of a day at the fair.

Pulled Pork on Biscuits with Coleslaw

Serves 4 generously

If you have leftover Roasted Pork Shoulder (page 200), this is the thing to make; but I find myself roasting pork with this in mind. A bottle of Rolling Rock Sauce (page 276) spices the pork up a bit.

FOR THE COLESLAW

½ medium red cabbage, cored, halved, and sliced as thinly as possible

3 medium carrots, scrubbed and grated (use a large-holed box grater)

1 jalapeño, trimmed, halved, seeded, and slivered

1 bunch scallions, trimmed and slivered

Kosher salt

2 tablespoons red wine vinegar

3 tablespoons Aioli (page 34) or mayonnaise

About 1 teaspoon Tabasco sauce

FOR THE PORK AND BISCUITS

1 pound Roasted Pork Shoulder (page 200)

About 3 cups Rolling Rock Sauce (page 276) or other barbecue sauce, optional

8 Savory Biscuits (page 274)

Make the coleslaw. Combine the cabbage, carrots, jalapeño, and scallions in a bowl. Season with salt, mix thoroughly, and set aside for 15 minutes. In a small bowl, mix the vinegar with the aioli. Add the Tabasco (more or less if you like) and mix well. Add the dressing to the slaw, mix, and let stand for 10 minutes.

Pull the pork, warm the biscuits, and assemble. If you are starting with leftover pork, put it in an ovenproof skillet or baking dish with a little water, cover tightly with foil, and heat in a 325°F oven until the meat is warmed through, about 25 minutes. Shred ("pull") the warm pork with two forks and season with Rolling Rock sauce if desired. Keep warm.

Meanwhile, heat the biscuits in the 325°F oven for about 15 minutes. Cut the biscuits in half, fill with pulled pork and coleslaw, and serve with more Rolling Rock Sauce if you like.

Savory Biscuits

Makes 10

Start with cold ingredients and don't overwork this savory variation of the biscuit dough I use for shortcake and cobbler.

> 2 cups all-purpose flour
>
> 1 tablespoon baking powder
>
> Pinch of salt
>
> 6 tablespoons cold butter, cubed
>
> 1 cup buttermilk
>
> 1 egg, beaten
>
> Sea salt and freshly ground pepper

Heat the oven to 400°F. Mix the flour, baking powder, and salt together in a large bowl. Using a pastry cutter or your fingers, work the butter into the flour mixture until the mixture looks like peas. Stir in the buttermilk.

Turn the dough out onto a lightly floured work surface and gather into a ball. Roll it about 1 inch thick, fold in half, then roll it again about 1 inch thick. Using a 2½-inch biscuit cutter (or highball glass), cut out 10 rounds and arrange on a baking sheet. Brush each biscuit with egg and sprinkle with sea salt and black pepper. Bake the biscuits, rotating the sheet once, until flaky and golden, about 20 minutes.

BURGERS

The first step toward a great hamburger is good meat. It needs to be flavorful and have some fat. With grass-fed beef, flavor isn't a problem, but having enough fat to keep things juicy can be. I don't want to have to grind meat to precise specifications, so I cheat and simply add some extra fat. I use chopped bone marrow, because the supermarket here carries soup bones year-round (you could use fatback instead). I chop ½ ounce (the amount from a good-sized bone) and mix it into 1 pound lean pasture-raised ground beef, add ½ teaspoon salt to the mix, and form 6-ounce patties.

I like burgers on the grill, but I also like them cooked on the stove in a skillet. Use a cast-iron pan and let it get really hot. Add a skim of oil, then add your patties. Let them sear for about 2 minutes, then lower the flame to medium and cook another minute or so. Flip the burgers and cook for about 3 minutes longer for medium-rare. When I imagine my perfect hamburger, condiments figure heavily in my fantasy. I want plenty of sliced tomatoes, Pickled Onions (page 282), Aioli (page 34), and Rolling Rock Sauce (below).

ROLLING ROCK SAUCE

We store this, my go-to sauce for burgers and pulled pork, in our "empties," hence the name for this beer-less condiment. Seed and chop a mixture of 12 hot and sweet peppers. Put them in a pot with 6 chopped tomatoes and 2 chopped onions. Add 2 cups malt vinegar and ¼ cup of pickling spice (you can make your own by combining 1 tablespoon each mustard seeds, coriander seeds, and allspice berries, with a pinch each crushed red pepper, ground ginger, and ground cinnamon, then adding a few cloves and a bay leaf). Add 2 tablespoons of Worcestershire and season lightly with salt. Bring the mixture to a boil, then reduce the heat and simmer until the vegetables blend to form a thick sauce, 2 to 3 hours. Puree the sauce in a food mill or food processor, then season with maple syrup and salt. Stored in sealed bottles in the refrigerator, Rolling Rock Sauce will last for months. This recipe makes enough to fill a six-pack.

Fried Squid and Onions

Serves 4

Sweet Vidalias are good in this recipe but not necessary—a little soak in milk takes enough sting out of any onion.

    1 medium onion, quartered through the stem, then sliced into
        crescents
    ½ cup milk
    Neutral oil, such as canola, for frying
    About 3 cups finely ground homemade bread crumbs
    Kosher salt
    Freshly ground black pepper
    About 1½ cups all-purpose flour
    2 eggs, beaten
    ½ pound cleaned squid, bodies and tentacles, bodies opened and
        cut into lengths about the size of the onion slices

Combine the onion and milk in a small bowl and set aside for 20 minutes.

Organize yourself for frying. Heat about 2 inches oil in a deep skillet or large saucepan over medium-high heat. Put the bread crumbs on a plate and season with salt and pepper. Put the flour on another plate and the eggs in a shallow bowl.

Fry the onions first. Drain them, then working in batches of a few slices at a time, dip first in the flour, then in the egg, then in the bread crumbs. Shake off any excess, add to the hot oil, and fry until crisp on all sides, about 1 minute per batch. With a slotted spoon or a pair of tongs, transfer the onions to paper towels to drain and sprinkle with salt while they are hot.

Fry the squid. Discard the leftover egg and flour. Again working in small batches, roll pieces of the squid in the bread crumbs, coating them completely. Add the squid to the hot oil and fry, turning them so they cook evenly, until they are crisp, about 30 seconds per batch. Drain and salt the squid. Serve the fried squid and onions together while they are hot.

Fish Tostados

Serves 4 as a first course or snack

You could use store-bought tortillas — but don't. Make your own; it makes a world of difference and it is easy. You don't need a tortilla press, just a rolling pin. Pulled Pork (page 273) is also a great filling for tostados.

FOR THE TORTILLAS

½ cup masa harina (see Note on page 281)

Kosher salt

Neutral oil, such as canola, for frying (use the same oil to fry the fish)

FOR THE CABBAGE

1½ cups shredded green cabbage

Juice of ½ lemon

Kosher salt

FOR THE DRESSING

¼ cup crème fraîche or sour cream

About 1 teaspoon minced jalapeño

½ teaspoon chopped pickled jalapeño, plus 1 teaspoon of the pickling liquid

1 scallion, trimmed, white part only, thinly sliced

Kosher salt

FOR THE FISH

About 2 cups all-purpose flour

1 egg

About ⅓ pound flounder or sole fillet, portioned into 4 pieces

Kosher salt

FOR THE TOSTADOS

½ cup Pickled Onions (page 282) or sliced scallions

¼ cup fresh cilantro leaves

1 lemon, halved

1 lime, cut into wedges

Pickled jalapeños, for garnish (optional)

Make the tortilla dough. Combine the masa harina and a pinch of salt in a bowl. Mix in about 5 tablespoons of warm water—enough so the dough is moist and pliable. Knead the dough until it is smooth, then gather it into a ball, wrap in plastic, and refrigerate for at least 30 minutes.

Form and cook the tortillas. Divide the dough into fourths. Working one at a time, place a portion of dough between two pieces of plastic wrap—this keeps the dough from sticking. Flatten each piece into a disc (if your dough is dry and crumbly don't hesitate to knead in a drop or two of water), then roll into a thin 4-inch round. Heat a heavy-bottomed skillet over medium heat. Toast the tortillas, 1 or 2 at a time, until they no longer stick to the pan, about 40 seconds. Flip and cook until the second side is toasted, about 40 seconds. (At this point the cooked tortillas can be used to make tacos; if this is your plan, wrap them in a towel and put in a warm oven until you are ready to serve.) For tostados, put the toasted tortillas on a plate to dry out a little before you fry them.

Prepare the cabbage. Put the shredded cabbage in a bowl. Add the lemon juice and some salt, mix well, and set aside for 20 minutes or so.

Prepare the dressing. Combine the crème fraîche, fresh and pickled jalapeño, pickling liquid, and scallion in a bowl. Season with salt, mix well, and reserve.

Fry the tortillas. Just before you plan to serve, heat a generous inch of neutral oil in a skillet over medium-high heat. When the oil shimmers, add the tortillas and fry 1 or 2 at a time until crisp, 2 minutes per side. Drain on a plate lined with paper towels. Keep the oil hot to fry the fish.

Fry the fish. Divide the flour between two plates. Beat the egg with a teaspoon of water in a bowl. Working with one piece at a time, dip the fish into the flour on the first plate, then into the egg, then into the flour on the second plate. Shake to loosen the excess flour, then add the fish to the oil, a few pieces at a time, and fry (still over medium-high heat), turning once, until golden on both sides, about 3 minutes. Transfer to a plate lined with paper towels to drain and season with salt while still hot.

Assemble the tostados. Spoon some dressing onto each tortilla. Top with cabbage, pickled onions, cilantro, and then the fish. Squeeze a bit of lemon on the fish. Serve with lime wedges, extra dressing, and pickled jalapeños if desired.

Note: Masa harina is very fine flour made from corn that has been dried, cooked with "lime water" (calcium hydroxide), finely ground, and dried again, using an ages-old method. Cornmeal is not a substitute.

Pickled Onions

Makes 1 cup

I like to double or even quadruple this recipe — it's easy and these onions are good on almost everything.

1 large onion, sliced across the grain

1 heaping tablespoon coriander seeds

1 heaping tablespoon kosher salt

1 heaping tablespoon black peppercorns

1 star anise

About ½ cup white vinegar

Bring several cups of water to a boil in a pan over high heat. Put the onion in an 8-ounce jar (with a lid). Pour just enough of the boiling water over the onion to half fill the jar. Add the coriander, salt, peppercorns, and star anise, then add enough vinegar to fill the jar. Tighten the lid and gently shake the jar to dissolve the salt. Let sit out for 2 hours, then refrigerate. These keep for months.

Corn in the Coals with Spiced Sage Butter

Serves 4

Freshly picked corn cooks very quickly. Older corn, no longer quite as full of sugar, will take a little longer. I like to rub the corn with some lively tasting dried, ground chili pepper. I tried, and liked, Aleppo pepper recently—you can find it at well-stocked spice stores and Middle Eastern markets.

8 fresh sage leaves

4 tablespoons butter

Kosher salt

Pinch cayenne, paprika, or other spicy ground chili pepper, such as Aleppo

About 1 tablespoon freshly squeezed lime juice

4 ears corn, husked

Build a fire in a grill and let it burn down to hot coals. Put the sage leaves in a small skillet and toast them over the fire until they are fragrant, about 3 minutes. Take the pan off the heat. When the sage is cool enough to handle, chop or crumble the leaves and return to the pan. Add the butter, a little salt, and the ground chili pepper. Set the skillet back on the grill and allow the butter to melt. Add lime juice to taste.

Put the ears of corn directly on the coals. Use tongs to turn them so they brown evenly on all sides, about 2 minutes. Pull the corn out of the fire; brush it with the sage butter, and serve.

Gaga's Blackberry Pie

Makes 1 (10-inch) pie

I agree with my grandmother's choice of tapioca—it thickens without flavoring and doesn't wind up gummy. I use minute tapioca pearls and let them macerate with the berries and sugar until they dissolve.

FOR THE DOUGH
2½ cups all-purpose flour

1 tablespoon sugar

Pinch of salt

½ pound (2 sticks) cold butter, cut into pieces

About ½ cup ice water

FOR THE FILLING
6 cups blackberries

½ cup sugar

3 tablespoons minute whole tapioca pearls

1 egg, beaten

Make the dough. Combine the flour, sugar, and salt in a bowl (or in a food processor). Cut the butter into the dry ingredients by hand with a pastry cutter (or by pulsing a few times in the machine). When the butter is pea sized, mix in just enough ice water so the dough comes together. Divide the dough in half and shape it into 2 discs. Wrap in plastic and refrigerate for at least 1 hour.

Make the filling. Combine the berries, sugar, and tapioca in a bowl. Toss to mix, then set aside to macerate until the sugar and tapioca dissolve, about 20 minutes.

Finish the pie. Heat the oven to 400°F. Roll out one piece of dough on a lightly floured work surface to a 14-inch round. Fit the dough into a 10-inch pie plate. Roll out the second piece of dough to a 12-inch round. Spoon the berries into the pie shell and top with the second dough round. Seal and crimp the edges. Using a sharp knife, cut 5 or 6 vents into the top crust. Brush the top with the beaten egg.

Put the pie on a baking sheet and bake until the crust begins to color, about 15 minutes. Reduce the heat to 325°F and bake until the crust is golden and the filling is bubbling through the vents, about 45 minutes more. Cool, slice, and serve.

Acknowledgments

I must begin by thanking my family. My mom taught me to dream big and never to be afraid to wander outside the lines, and my dad showed me that working hard is the secret to a well-lived life. He learned this from his father. I want to thank Poppy for that, and to thank him and Gaga for creating and nurturing Beetlebung Farm so it could be the center of our life here. I also want to thank my aunt Marie Scott and her son Josh Scott. Marie worked with Poppy every summer and started our farm stand. Josh generously offers me his support and provides us with incredible meat from his herds.

This book would not exist but for the help of everyone at Little, Brown. I want to especially thank editor-in-chief Judy Clain for her faith in me, and my editors, Michael Sand and Michael Szczerban, for their guidance. Michael Sand steered me through the process of creating a book, beat me at Ping-Pong, and brought my words to the page. I would also like to thank Garrett McGrath and my agent, Steve Troha. Many thanks to my friend Tamara Weiss, who supported me and introduced me to Judy and later to Cathy Young. Cathy listened, helped me frame what I wanted to say, and, best of all, became my friend over the course of our year working together. Photographer Gabriela Herman and letterpress artist Emma Young are responsible for the art in this book. I must thank Gab for always sharing her talent and flair. And thank Emma for helping me realize my vision through her tireless work and with her simple, beautiful art. I also want to thank Hannah Leighton, who lent her wonderful energy to this endeavor, and Lee Desrosiers, who shared his considerable skill in the kitchen. I am deeply grateful to Olivia Pattison, an amazing pastry chef, who helped create the sweets for this book. Kayla Foster and Elana Carlson helped keep me on track and I am grateful to them both. I am also grateful to Sarah and Bob Nixon, the owners of the Beach Plum Inn & Restaurant; they allowed me to work in my own idiosyncratic way. I also want to express special appreciation to Jason Nichols, Kristina Almquist, Remy Tumin, Kathryn Arffa, Linda Lipsett, Ellen Poss, and my pal Luke Weinstock.

Every time I sit down at my desk I feel grateful to all my teachers. They taught me to love words and gave me the confidence to tell my story. I'm indebted to Julia Wells, the editor of the *Vineyard Gazette,* for printing my essays about this island I love. Finally, I want to thank the farmers. Farming is at the heart of this island and all I do. I want to salute all the island growers, those who have been working their land for decades, and those who have come more recently to raise food. Thank you for everything you have shared and all that I continue to learn from each of you.

METRIC CONVERSIONS

VOLUME

FORMULAS

Cups to milliliters — multiply by 2.4

Cups to liters — multiply cups by .24

EXACT EQUIVALENTS

1 teaspoon .... 4.9 milliliters

1 tablespoon ....14.8 milliliters

1 ounce .... 29.57 milliliters

1 cup .... 236.6 milliliters

1 pint .... 473.2 milliliters

APPROXIMATE EQUIVALENTS

¼ cup .... 60 milliliters

⅓ cup .... 80 milliliters

½ cup ....120 milliliters

⅔ cup .... 160 milliliters

¾ cup .... 177 milliliters

1 cup .... 230 milliliters

1¼ cups .... 300 milliliters

1½ cups .... 360 milliliters

1⅔ cups .... 400 milliliters

2 cups .... 460 milliliters

2½ cups .... 600 milliliters

3 cups .... 700 milliliters

4 cups (1 quart) .... .95 liter

4 quarts (1 gallon) .... 3.8 liters

WEIGHT

FORMULAS

Ounces to grams — multiply ounces by 28.35

Pounds to grams — multiply pounds by 453.5

Pounds to kilograms — multiply pounds by .45

EXACT EQUIVALENTS

1 ounce .... 28.35 grams

1 pound .... 453.59 grams, .45 kilograms

APPROXIMATE EQUIVALENTS (WEIGHT)

¼ ounce .... 7 grams

½ ounce .... 14 grams

1 ounce .... 28 grams

1¼ ounces .... 35 grams

1½ ounces .... 40 grams

1⅔ ounces .... 45 grams

2 ounces .... 55 grams

2½ ounces .... 70 grams

4 ounces .... 112 grams

5 ounces .... 140 grams

8 ounces .... 228 grams

10 ounces .... 280 grams

15 ounces .... 425 grams

16 ounces (1 pound) .... 454 grams

TEMPERATURE

FORMULA

Fahrenheit to centigrade — subtract 32 from
Fahrenheit, multiply by 5, then divide by 9
(F–32) x 5/9

APPROXIMATE EQUIVALENTS

250°F .... 120°C

275°F .... 135°C

300°F .... 150°C

325°F .... 160°C

350°F .... 180°C

375°F .... 190°C

400°F .... 200°C

450°F .... 230°C

LENGTH

FORMULA

Inches to centimeters — multiply inches by 2.54

RECISE LIST

Each chapter of this book contains a menu. The menus are progressions that appeal to me, but it is my hope that you will take the dishes that I have gathered and work them into your own routines and celebrations. To make that easier, I've listed all my recipes—the book at a glance—grouping them by principal ingredient (meat, fish, and vegetables), with the appetizers listed first in each group, followed by the entrees. I have separately noted pasta and crostini, drinks, desserts, breakfast dishes, and sauces.

MEAT AND FOWL

FISH AND SEAFOOD

VEGETABLES

CROSTINI, GRAINS, AND PASTA

SAUCES AND PICKLES

DRINKS

DESSERTS

BREAKFAST

INDEX

ABOUT THE AUTHOR

Chris Fischer was born on Martha's Vineyard, unlike his older brother Andrew, who was born in Falmouth and will always be a wash-ashore.

Catherine Young grew up spending summers on Martha's Vineyard. She practiced law before entering the food world. She cooked at leading restaurants, including Union Square Café, Lespinasse, and Gramercy Tavern, worked as an editor at *Saveur* magazine, and coauthored *Think Like a Chef* and *The Craft of Cooking*, both with Tom Colicchio; *Anatomy of a Dish* with Diane Forley; and *Salt to Taste: Keys to Confident Delicious Cooking* with Marco Canora. Cathy lives with her husband and daughter in Brooklyn.

Gabriela Herman is a photographer based in Brooklyn and on Martha's Vineyard. Her personal work has been exhibited internationally and she's a regular contributor to magazines around the globe.

Emma Young is a designer, printmaker, and poet who works primarily in typeset letterpress. She is a born-and-raised islander and farmer, and continues to live and work in West Tisbury.

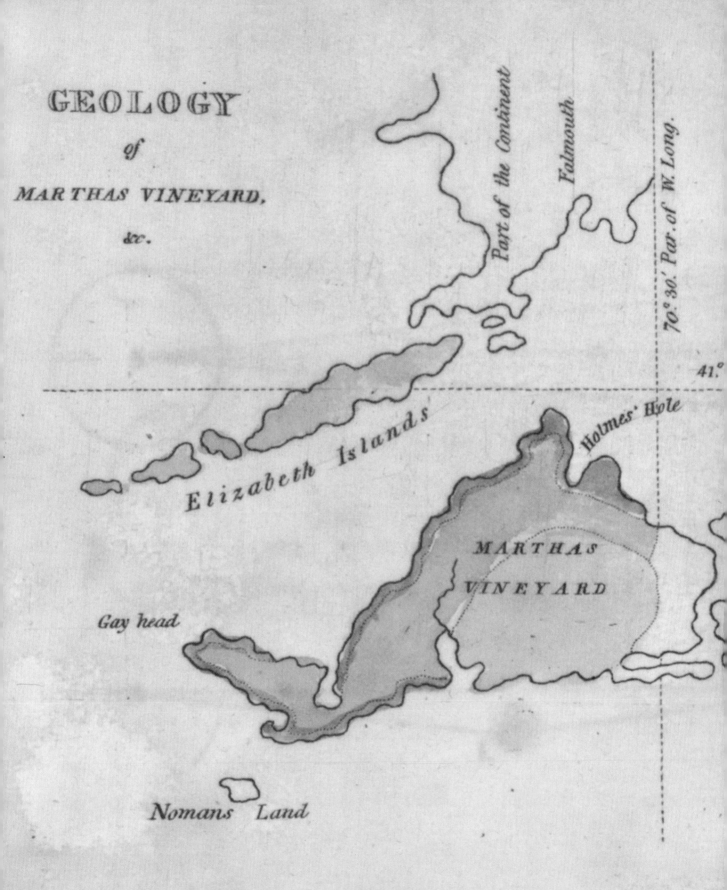